Praise for *Smarter Se*

'Every now and then, you read a book that turns accepted wisdom on its head and shows a new way. This is one of those books.'
Rick Adkinson, CEO, Private Capital

'The new approaches to building better relationships and the practical steps outlined in this book were a big hit with our members.'
Simon Twiston-Davies, CEO, The Cable and Satellite Broadcasting Association of Asia (CASBAA)

'*Smarter Selling* lifts the lid on manipulative sales approaches and shows how to build long-term trusted relationships that deliver greater value to all.'
Robert Agnew, Managing Director, Matrix Services (Hong Kong, Shanghai and Mumbai)

'The tools this book introduces and the mindset change it drives will make a significant impact on the relationship and sales success of most organisations.'
Peter Savoff, General Manager, Hotels, Anthony John Group

'If your organisation relies on deep and sustainable relationships to drive profits, then applying the methods outlined in this book will undoubtedly contribute to better performance.'
Paul Hodgson, Founder and Managing Director, Sustainnovation Pty Ltd

'We've been working with the authors for the last four years, introducing their ideas and approaches to our people. Without a doubt this has helped us build stronger customer relationships.'
Jeannie Luk, Regional Training & Development Director, China, Schenker-BAX

'If you liked SPIN Selling, you should read *Smarter Selling*. This book completes the jigsaw of buyer influences through addressing the emotional and psychological aspects of the sales process. This critical dimension provides a means for real differentiation.'
Chris Greaves, Sales Director (Northern Europe), Ipswitch Inc.

'A very practical guide to building lasting high-value relationships. The book is easy to read and especially helpful in mapping out the thought process and the actions required – complete with guides and planning sheets. An indispensable tool for consultants and salespeople.'

Iain Brown, Managing Director, ATP Fire and Security Group

Smarter Selling

FT Prentice Hall
FINANCIAL TIMES

In an increasingly competitive world, we believe it's quality of thinking that gives you the edge – an idea that opens new doors, a technique that solves a problem, or an insight that simply makes sense of it all. The more you know, the smarter and faster you can go.

That's why we work with the best minds in business and finance to bring cutting-edge thinking and best learning practice to a global market.

Under a range of leading imprints, including *Financial Times Prentice Hall*, we create world-class print publications and electronic products bringing our readers knowledge, skills and understanding, which can be applied whether studying or at work.

To find out more about Pearson Education publications, or tell us about the books you'd like to find, you can visit us at
www.pearsoned.co.uk

Pearson Education

Keith Dugdale and
David Lambert

Smarter
Selling

Next generation sales strategies to meet your
buyer's needs – every time

 Prentice Hall

FINANCIAL TIMES

An imprint of Pearson Education

Harlow, England ■ London ■ New York ■ Toronto Sydney ■ Tokyo ■ Singapore
Hong Kong ■ Cape Town ■ New Delhi ■ Madrid ■ Paris ■ Amsterdam ■ Munich ■ Milan

PEARSON EDUCATION LIMITED

Edinburgh Gate
Harlow CM20 2JE
Tel: +44 (0)1279 623623
Fax: +44 (0)1279 431059
Website: www.pearsoned.co.uk

First published in Great Britain in 2007

ISBN: 978 0 273 71246 6

British Library Cataloguing-in-Publication Data
A catalogue record for this book is available from the British Library

10   9   8   7   6   5   4   3   2
11   10   09   08   07

Typeset in Stone Serif 9 point by 3
Printed and bound in Great Britain by Ashford Colour Press Ltd, Gosport

The publisher's policy is to use paper manufactured from sustainable forests.

For Soraya and Shaila

Contents

Acknowledgements

This book is the result of more than 20 years of working and teaching in sales and marketing. Years spent observing sales behaviours, extracting successful patterns, codifying them and testing them on willing clients.

To all those willing clients and to all our colleagues who gave us help and support along the way, a big thank you.

We all have mentors. People we admire. People we learn from. People who are there with the advice we need, even when we may not want to hear it. Neil Wilson, Chris Reardon, Robert Gazzi, Robert Sandry, Simon Fitzgeorge and Ken Everett are such people. Gentlemen it has been a pleasure.

In finalising the manuscript we are grateful for the input of clients, friends and family. Please forgive us if we did not implement all your advice and be assured that all advice was considered!

We must also thank Think on Your Feet International, Inc., not only for educating us in the most effective communications techniques we have come across, but also for allowing us to share some of their ideas with you in this book.

Finally and most importantly to our families. To our parents and siblings who shaped our early thinking and still support us today. To our wives who stand with us every step of the way and to our children who together give our lives meaning. We dedicate this book to you.

Copyright

Think on Your Feet® is a registered trademark of Think on Your Feet International, Inc., and is registered with the U.S. Patent and Trademark Office, the Canadian Registrar of Trademarks, the Australian Trade Mark Office and the European Community.

About the authors

Keith Dugdale is an Australian-based specialist in human behaviour in the workplace. He has been focusing on the behavioural aspects of the sales process for more than a decade and is a consultant to individuals, local companies and global organisations.

Keith has lived and worked in many cultures including the UK, China, Singapore, Papua New Guinea, Africa, Hong Kong and Australia. He has held senior positions in people development and business development.

Keith now tries to get a balance between looking after his wife and three children in Australia and running a global business helping people succeed in selling.

David Lambert is a Hong Kong-based communicatons and training consultant. He began to specialise in communications more than 15 years ago and since then has been a consultant to many leading companies and government bodies – helping them improve their internal and external communications.

David has held senior positions in business development, marketing, communicatons and training and development.

He now devotes his professional time to delivering communications training programmes and coaching executives to improve their presentation style; and divides his personal time amongst his wife, two children and his love of soccer!

They have both invested much of their working lives building the portfolio of concepts and tools outlined in this book, but until recently have never found the time to take their feet off the accelerator pedal long enough to sit back and write it all down.

So, some 40 years after each started his own learning journey and 20 years after they started applying the learning in a work environment, they eventually put pen to paper.

What finally got them to do it? Their wives. They could only take so many back-handed comments about the infamous, ground-breaking epic that was never written.

Introduction

Everyone sells. Some people sell ideas, some sell services and some sell products. Whatever you sell, this book will help you do it better, and feel better about doing it.

Smarter Selling is a distillation of the authors' many years' experience working with all types of salespeople and consultants in a broad range of industries, from accounting and legal, through banking and insurance, management consultancy, IT, sports, transport, media, and many aspects of retail. It describes the mindset adopted by truly consultative salespeople – those who sustain long-term, mutually beneficial relationships with key buyers – and it details an approach, coupled with a series of easy-to-learn tools that drive sales relationships towards sustainable, trusted partnerships.

How is *Smarter Selling* different to other sales books?

Many sales methodologies, including some that claim to be consultative in nature, focus on helping the salesperson identify a problem that is addressed by their service or product, in order that they can make a sale. Sometimes this works for the seller and the buyer, but often the buyer is persuaded to purchase something that they do not really need, with the result that the salesperson succeeds in the short term, but risks souring the long-term relationship.

Smarter Selling outlines a different sales journey. A journey that progresses at a natural pace, where buyer and seller collaborate, with the seller facilitating the buyer's thought process and helping them achieve their goals. This results in a sales experience that the buyer enjoys rather than endures, that is recognised as different, and that the buyer wants to repeat.

Smarter Selling adds a human dimension to the sales process, recognising that it is people who make buying decisions – and they make them based on instinct more often than intellect. As one sales director commented: 'Your approach provides the missing piece – the explanation for why we sometimes win jobs when our offering is similar to our competitors.'

Smarter Selling changes people. Buyers become more open and trusting – they share information freely and provide valuable citations and referrals. Colleagues and business associates share leads with you, safe in the knowledge that you will respect and honour their trust in you. You become more relaxed and confident, enjoying the selling process and the help you bring to your buyers.

Smarter Selling shows you the strategies to differentiate your sales approach through:

- recognising how you are perceived by others and being able to change that perception
- understanding the relationship you have with different buyers and knowing how to change the nature of those relationships
- understanding buyer types and roles and being able to adjust the approach needed for each different buyer
- identifying price-busters, deal-hunters and value-buyers, then allocating your precious time and energy more effectively
- initiating buyer interactions in a way that signals your clear focus on the buyer's needs
- engaging in a needs identification process that is open, free from manipulation and enjoyable for the buyer
- collaborating with your buyers jointly to identify and evaluate potential solutions
- presenting your ideas credibly and persuasively.

The impact is cumulative. Taken alone, each step represents a small piece of the process. Added together they represent a different, enjoyable and memorable buyer experience.

Smarter Selling contains important messages for many audiences including:

- anyone with a direct need to sell
- anyone responsible for a team or organisation that needs to sell
- anyone wanting to improve their own ability to develop deep business relationships
- anyone wanting to improve relationships within a team or organisation.

The approaches in this book have been applied across many industries and in more than 50 countries. Language is not an issue since it is people and how they think and behave that we are dealing with, not the words they use. Equally, although culture plays a part in the social norms of the sales interaction, particularly at the start, experience shows that these approaches are applicable across cultures.

How to use this book

The move to a true consultative selling approach is the hardest behavioural shift that most salespeople ever make. To aid this transition, we provide you with real-life examples, practice scenarios, self-tests and planning tools. We also give details of how to download additional resources from our web site at www.ioweu.com.

Certain chapters (1, 2, 3, 4 and 8) focus more on the mindset required. Other chapters (5, 6, 7 and 9) focus more on developing core skills. To practise the skills without developing the mindset is a sham. Buyers will see through it. Mindsets and skillsets must be aligned.

At the end of each chapter, the key points from that chapter are summarised. These are collated in Chapter 11, to provide a thumbnail sketch and *aide-mémoire* of the book's key messages.

Throughout the book we track the progress of Richard and Emily, two salespeople wrestling with the challenges of selling in today's environment. Through their experiences and development, we see the application and impact of our concepts and tools. As with the movies, the actions of this fictional couple bear no relationship to any individuals either living or dead! However, their actions and the results of those actions are based on real events that we have either experienced or observed.

Let us introduce you to them now.

Richard and Emily of FuturePerfect Systems are very successful sales people. They have been selling FuturePerfect's Apostle software for 15 years.

With the increased capabilities of technology and the changing demands of customers the software has been adapted over the years. It has always been seen by the market as slightly ahead of competitor products.

Apostle is an integrated back office system with five 'Manager'

▶

modules: Inventory Manager, Logistics Manager, Sales Manager, People Manager and Accounts Manager. Customers who do not need the whole package can purchase individual modules. One of its greatest attributes is that it can be scaled according to the needs of each customer.

When Richard and Emily started out in the early 1990s, they worked hard to really understand their product and spent a lot of time researching their target company. Their success rate was significantly higher than most competitors. This was partly down to their product but also down to the fact that they were very good salespeople. They had a reputation as closers of deals and also had a very effective way of dealing with objections. They negotiated hard and rarely had to discount.

All in all a success story.

In the late 1990s Richard and Emily noticed that their success rates seemed to slip a little. Buyers were still buying, but their competitors seemed to be having more success. It did not appear to be about the product – it still compared very favourably to the competition. They decided that maybe it was just that other salespeople were doing something better. Although it hurt their pride somewhat they started to read books and attend programmes on selling skills.

Richard and Emily realised that what they were still doing was selling their product on its own merits with little regard to the buyer. They were still expecting an instant sale, and if they did not get it they would move on to the next target. The reading and training helped them adapt a more consultative approach to selling.

They became better at focusing on the buyer and learned some very sophisticated questioning techniques. These techniques moved them in their buyers' eyes from being salespeople to being consultants. Yes they still focused on questioning a buyer about the issue that might highlight the buyer's need for their product, but they focused the process on questions rather than statement.

Their sales started to increase again, and the need for discounts reduced. They were back on track. As an insight to their approach take a look at their meeting planning form.

Buyer company name		Buyer individual name	
Industry		Turnover	
Economic or user buyer		Contact history	
How our product might fit		Why it might fit	
Questions to ask at next meeting to uncover buyer need for our product			
Deadlines for stop/go decision on sale			

The late 1990s and the early years of the new century proved to be the best years of Richard and Emily's careers. Sales were booming. Regardless of the increased sales targets allocated to them they always met or even exceeded them.

Then, in early 2006, buyers seemed to start challenging their product more. They started to push back on the price again. It was harder to get meetings and even buyers who had bought from them before and been happy with the product wanted them to go through a full proposal process in competition with others. These competitive proposal processes took up so much of their time that they barely had the time, or energy, to knock on new doors. Some buyers even outsourced the proposal process to a third party – thus making the sale even more driven by product and price.

Richard and Emily started to offer 'freebies' as a way of increasing their chances of a win. To a certain extent this worked where there was no proposal but had no impact on the more painful proposal processes.

Something needed to give. Either their price needed to drop or they needed a new approach. Maybe, thought Richard, it was time to move on. Then Emily picked up a copy of *Smarter Selling* at Frankfurt airport. . .

If you identify at all with Richard and Emily, then this book is for you. As you follow their progress, you will uncover the awareness, the strategies and the tools to be more successful – to sell smarter. Your buyers will experience the change; your bosses will observe the results; and you will reap the benefits.

1

I Owe U – next generation sales strategies

'Be the change you want to see in the world.'

Mahatma Gandhi (1869–1948)

There is a saying, often heard in business, that the only constant is change. The way that people sell their ideas, services and products – both within and outside organisations – must change too. In this chapter, we outline the challenges faced by sellers today, and an approach to modern complex sales that transforms the sales journey and moves the buyer–seller relationship to new levels of trust and collaboration.

Stately Homes – part 1

Richard and Emily had been trying for weeks to arrange a meeting with Peter Leung, IT Manager at Stately Homes, a company they were keen to do business with.

Emily had learned that Stately were using an outdated inventory management system and she knew that FuturePerfect's Apostle software was far superior. She was bringing Richard with her to the meeting because he had a better knowledge of the Apostle system specifications.

After finally persuading Peter Leung to set aside an hour to see her, Emily had worked hard to put together a comprehensive slide pack demonstrating FuturePerfect's capabilities and the Apostle inventory management software. She had prepared a meeting agenda and sent

▶

it to Mr Leung. He had made no changes – everything was looking good.

Peter Leung's secretary met Richard and Emily at the reception area and led them to Stately's boardroom.

Mr Leung arrived and two colleagues were waiting for them, saying they were interested to hear more about FuturePerfect and the Apostle system.

Emily spoke for 10 minutes, introducing herself and Richard, describing their experience and telling the story of FuturePerfect's development into a leading bespoke software developer. She then handed over to Richard who presented for 20 minutes on the features of the Apostle system, focusing on the key areas where Apostle was superior to Stately's current system.

Richard took slightly longer to cover his part than Emily had expected, but he provided a lot of information. Mr Leung thanked them for their comprehensive presentation and said he would consider their suggestions.

Emily asked if he needed more information and explained there was a special discount available to customers who purchased the standard system before the end of the month. She also offered to arrange for Mr Leung to speak to other Apostle users so that he could satisfy himself as to the superior features of the system.

Mr Leung then ended the meeting saying that he had an important appointment at the other side of town and needed to leave soon. He would call them once he had consulted with his colleagues.

As far as Emily and Richard were concerned everything had gone as well as it could. They had covered everything they wanted and there were no objections. The meeting had only ended because Mr Leung had another important meeting to attend.

Consequently, they were very surprised when, a few minutes later as they sat in the building's coffee shop, they saw Mr Leung coming back into the office with what looked like his lunch.

1.1 Selling today

Much of the selling that is done today focuses on persuading people to buy things that they might not really need, at least not yet. Cut-throat pricing, fierce competition and high, short-term sales targets drive salespeople to behave in ways that can be painful for buyers – and often uncomfortable for the salesperson too.

To understand this better, we asked the salespeople that we worked with to tell us how they are currently perceived by the buyers they work with. Then we asked them how they would like to be perceived. The results were remarkably consistent across different industries and we think they neatly summarise the challenges facing salespeople today. We've reproduced them in the table overleaf.

Next, we asked ourselves how they had arrived at their current situation.

We realised that many salespeople still learned their craft from colleagues or from training programmes that were designed for an earlier time or for selling relatively simple, low-cost products – mostly in a consumer environment. Sometimes, they simply thought about their experience of being sold to, and reflected this in the way they sold to others. Thus it is that the tactics and language of 'closing' and 'handling objections' developed for the US market in the mid-20th century persist today.

Examples of their continued use range from the shop assistant who tells you that every piece of clothing you try on looks fantastic on you; to the fitness guru's persuasion that 15 minutes each day will give you dream abdominals; and even to the IT companies who argue that installing their networked database system will mean that all your employees will suddenly change the way they work and become hugely collaborative, sharing all the knowledge and expertise that they have guarded so jealously for years.

It is more common these days to encounter these tactics in low-cost, high-volume environments, such as raw materials and components, office supplies and transportation, where the product or service is seen as a commodity and the buyer's primary decision-making criteria is price.

By contrast, complex business transactions that involve significant cost and higher potential risk to the buyer demand a different approach. As Neil Rackham revealed in his ground-breaking book *SPIN Selling* (1988), the tactics that delivered sales success in small value or simple sales did not work for complex, high-value sales.

Sellers' possible challenges	Current situation	Desired position	Value in achieving the desired outcome
Competition	Buyers see me as one of many – someone with a commodity, product or service. They only talk to me about my specific offering and then only if I chase them. Price is the major determinant of whether they buy. I spend a lot of time chasing leads. I submit lots of proposals.	Buyers want to talk to me. They suggest new products or services that I can develop which might help them. I am the natural provider of my offering. Price is a secondary concern. Value is more important. Fewer proposals. Demand driven.	More profitable and enjoyable assignments.
Shallow relationships	Buyers only talk to me when they have a need for my offering or when I think they have a need for it. A defined beginning and end to each assignment. They jump on the smallest mistake. Need to re-propose every time. Product management and pipeline management seem to fill my day.	Buyers trust me and look for my opinion on matters other than my core offering. There is no defining start or end to a project – it is an ongoing relationship. They forgive my mistakes, and they don't get hung up on price. I spend nearly all my time doing what I want to do not what I have to do.	Fewer, but deeper relationships where we enjoy working together. Huge long-term profitability.
Confidence	I worry about whether I have done enough research. I worry about someone else knowing more than I do. I worry about whether the product is good enough. I worry about where the next sale is coming from. I worry about having to contact people I don't know or am not sure about.	I have inner confidence in my ability to help people. I am less concerned with having to know the answer.	Significant reduction in stress and increase in fun and personal satisfaction. Less time researching.

Rackham discovered that for success in larger, more complex sales, the salesperson had to work to develop a deep understanding of the problems facing the customer before outlining the benefits of their service or product in solving the problem. In this way the salesperson was seen to behave more like a consultant. Thus was born the term 'consultative selling'.

Interestingly, despite Rackham's insights, many salespeople still struggle to listen to buyers before they introduce their product or service.

In one of those moments where everything suddenly comes together, we were once running training sessions for a client and happened upon the perfect real-life illustration to demonstrate to our trainees the need to listen to buyers.

As we got into the elevator at lunch, together with some of the trainees, two clients of the company also got into our lift. One of the clients was purple with anger. We cannot repeat his language here, but what he muttered as steam came out of his ears was something like, 'Why don't these people ever ******* listen to us?'

The consultative sales process is generally less painful for the buyer than having a product or service pushed at them. For the salesperson, it can be more painful – or at least more difficult – since they need better developed questioning skills and a sound knowledge of the buyer's business if they are to engage in a meaningful conversation about the buyer's needs.

But this process is often manipulative. The salesperson still enters the relationship with a singular focus – to identify the buyer's need that fits with their offering. This aim drives them to certain undesirable behaviours.

A client of ours, at board level in a large global organisation, commented to us recently that while it was interesting how many of the professionals he met had improved in the way that they sold, at the end of the day, they still did not get it right. 'They ask one really good question,' he said, 'and then their eyes glaze over as they wait for an opportunity to sell their offering'.

1.2 Next generation selling

The next generation selling approach this book is based around is called 'I Owe U'. It is a new approach that moves consultative selling to a new dimension – a dimension that the word 'consultative' suggests, but that in practice is not always achieved. Second generation consultative selling establishes a similar level of trust between buyer and seller as exists between doctor and patient.

The I Owe U approach demands a 180-degree flip in the buyer–seller relationship. It starts with the premise that rather than the buyer owing the salesperson an order, the salesperson owes the buyer.

Why do they owe the buyer? Because the buyer is investing time in meeting the salesperson. Because the buyer is asked to reveal information about their organisation – some of which may be sensitive or even painful to discuss. Because at some point the buyer may even commit to a purchase. Surely this investment – real and potential – merits some reward.

The reward is easily given and valued by the buyer, but strangely is insufficiently valued and rarely offered by the seller. Perhaps because it is intangible. Typically the reward revolves around shared knowledge, shared experience and shared contacts.

The few who recognise the debt and seek to give the reward, enjoy deeper, more trusted relationships with their buyers.

I Owe U works best for sellers of complex, high-value products and services. Industries where I Owe U works well include:

- Technology – where salespeople can get carried away talking about detailed technical specifications, sometimes losing sight of the buyer's needs.

- Financial services – where organisations that offer a true personalised service, predicated on a deep understanding of the customer, outperform those that rely on gimmicks and promotions.

- Professional services – where status is underpinned by technical knowledge and consultants are reluctant to stray beyond the boundaries of their specialist area – even if the buyer's needs lie in another place.

Plus any other market where buyers are sophisticated and choice is wide. The point about buyer sophistication is important. Some organisations and some buyers do not want the kind of partnering relationship that I Owe U seeks to build. Investing too much time and energy into such relationships would be a mistake (see Chapters 3 and 4 for more on different relationships and buyer types), but equally, we should not dismiss such organisations since both people and organisations can change quickly – and with them their buying behaviours.

	Push	Consultative	Next generation (I Owe U)
The buyer is	■ an adversary to be overcome	■ a target to be persuaded	■ an individual to be respected
The salesperson talks about	■ the features of the product or service	■ the buyer's issues and how the product or service can help	■ the buyer's challenges and ideas for how to meet these challenges
Energy focused on	■ handling objections ■ closing the sale	■ escalating the need for action ■ matching your product or service to the problem ■ closing the sale	■ understanding the buyer's priorities ■ providing insights ■ deepening the relationship
Indicators of success	■ immediate sale	■ buyer's statement of need closely followed by sale	■ continued dialogue ■ continued expectation of sale at some future date
The salesperson has	■ the lines to open and close the sale	■ a process for uncovering and escalating needs	■ an intent to help and a process to develop rapport and understanding
The salesperson needs to know	■ their business and products	■ their business and products ■ the buyer's business and products	■ their business and products ■ the buyer's business and products; personal goals; and preferred working style

The time is right for I Owe U. Looking back, we can see that as competition increased, sales organisations seeking new ways to build customer loyalty and maintain profit margins looked towards high-earning consulting businesses and saw a model that they could copy.

But there was a problem. Many of the approaches bearing a consultative label turned out not to be genuinely consultative. They used clever words, but still focused on trying to help salespeople find a problem to fit their solution. In such scenarios the salesperson's task became to find what was causing pain to the buyer, then to 'push the bruise' to increase the pain, before offering their wonder drug as the only one that would magically take the pain away.

I Owe U is different, genuinely different. As with a doctor, the I Owe U salesperson recognises any pain, but then carefully diagnoses the full symptoms, working to understand the underlying causes. The prescribed remedy often involves a variety of treatments, some of which are self-administered, some that the doctor can administer and some that require the intervention of other specialists. So it is with the I Owe U salesperson. Their role is to help the buyer arrive at a set of actions that may or may not involve the salesperson's offerings, but for which they will be thanked, remembered – and trusted.

To see how I Owe U goes beyond 'push' and consultative selling, consider the table on p. 7.

1.3 The I Owe U sales journey

We think of the I Owe U sales experience as a journey. A journey that is quite different to most sales journeys in that it is longer and follows a quite different route.

The journey begins with the objective of helping the buyer improve the performance of their business. This objective is rooted in a belief that if the salesperson focuses on helping rather than selling, then in the long term, more sales will result.

This different mindset drives different behaviours. For example, for some salespeople, any opportunity to focus the conversation on areas favourable to their product or service is taken. When the buyer talks about the broader business challenges that they are facing, the salesperson is half-listening and half-thinking how this fits with their product or service. And, if it doesn't fit, they're thinking of ways that they can steer the conversation back to their preferred areas of interest.

We've worked with many organisations whose salespeople claim not to behave in this way; who claim to have excellent partnering relationships with their customers. Yet, the moment we observe them in a sales environment they fall into the trap of focusing the conversation on their organisation and their offering rather than the buyer's business and needs.

Indeed, one of the aspects of I Owe U that salespeople find most difficult is the maxim that you should talk about your organisation or offering *only* when the buyer asks you to – and then only if you have developed a good understanding of the buyer's needs. The trap mentioned in the previous paragraph is set by the question, often early in a meeting that goes something like:

'Thank you for coming to see me today. Can you start by telling me something about your company and its offerings?'

or more simply:

'What are you here to talk to me about?'

Those who fall into the trap respond by starting with a description of their organisation and their product or service, listing out the features and benefits of each. They do this because it is easy to do and comfortable. They've done it many times before. They can recite the words without even thinking about them – and that is where the problem starts. As soon as they begin to talk about themselves or their offering, they begin to sound like they are more interested in their own agenda, rather than their buyer's.

Faced with the question *'What are you here to talk to me about?'*, an I Owe U salesperson will pause and think before responding, will recognise that they cannot sensibly speak about how they would help the buyer until they know them better, and will avoid the trap. They might respond with something like:

'I could list all my offerings but they might be out of context with your needs. If you don't mind what I would like to do first is get a better understanding of any issues you may have. At that point I will be in a better position to know whether I can help you.'

They remember that the buyer has given the gift of time. They are giving information too and some of it may be sensitive, personal and confidential. You repay these gifts by listening to what they have to say, saying you want to understand and help by sharing your experience.

If we think of each conversation with the buyer as a journey, then each journey will be different. All buyers are different. All buying organisations are different. How can we expect that a one-size-fits-all approach can work? Surprisingly, some people do. They walk into a meeting with a standard sales pack and they present their ideas the same way, time after time, forcing the buyer to listen to their standard sales presentation.

> David was recently asked to coach a senior salesman who was having problems winning repeat business from his clients. The reason quickly became apparent – he was made of cardboard!
>
> He was chatty and outgoing, but all of his lines felt too rehearsed. This was confirmed when, asked how he responds to client requests for real-life examples of previous experience, he responded with a long explanation of the fact that he could not give examples for confidentiality reasons. He said that was his 'stock answer'.

A more experienced or sophisticated salesperson may not have a standard presentation, but they might still have their pre-prepared responses for any 'objections' that the buyer puts forward. Meetings tend to follow a linear pattern with the salesperson mentally ticking off the points they wanted to cover. To the buyer this can feel almost like an interrogation. It becomes very clear that the salesperson has a list of questions – in extreme cases a standard list of questions – and that they will force the conversation down certain routes to ensure that their points get made. The meeting progression could look something like that shown in Figure 1.1.

A person following the I Owe U approach would follow a less structured and usually non-linear route, allowing the buyer to dictate the flow of the meeting, focusing on listening to the buyer and sharing experience and insights.

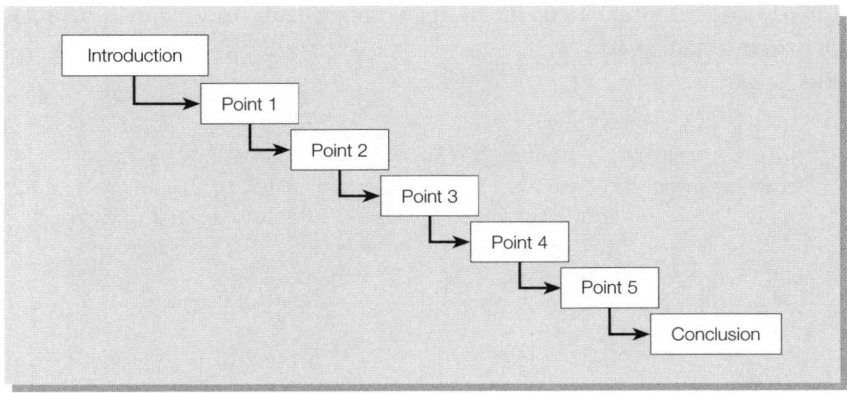

figure 1.1 Typical meeting progression

To start with, they are more likely to have five things they would like to understand about the buyer than five points they would like to make to the buyer. However, should they have five points to make, they could just make two or three of them during the meeting at appropriate times. Equally, they are just as likely to make none of the points they wanted to make and instead will simply listen to the buyer.

I Owe U meetings follow a circuitous and unpredictable route – with control resting with the buyer, not the seller (see Figure 1.2).

Any points not covered can be picked up and dealt with at the end of the meeting or covered in a later conversation. The buyer, grateful for the

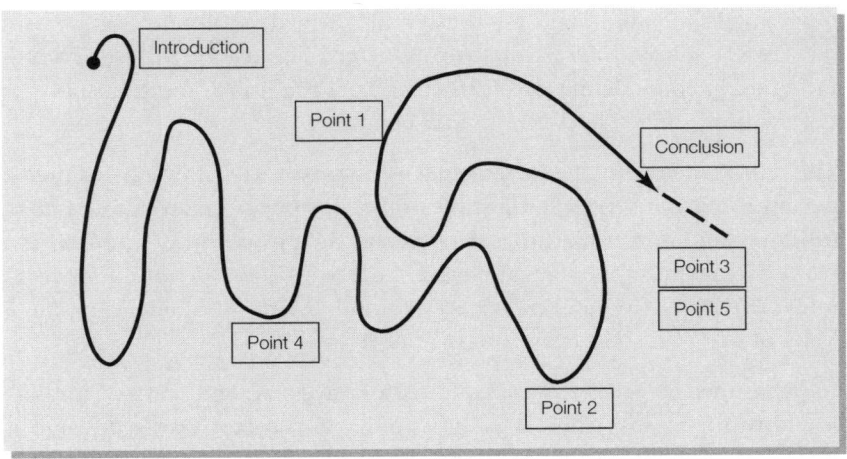

figure 1.2 An I Owe U meeting

interest and attention that the salesperson has demonstrated, will be quite prepared to talk again.

> Karl, a tax expert, is meeting the finance director of a major company to discuss a complex tax issue. He has some points he needs to cover, but as he enters the meeting he notices that his client appears restless and agitated. He comments on this and asks the client if he wants to cover the tax issue today or whether he has something else to deal with that is more urgent.
>
> The client explains that a key member of his finance team in China has just resigned and that he needs to be replaced very quickly, but they are struggling to find someone. Karl suggests that his company may be able to help, as they provide assistance with recruitment and they have offices in China. The client is both pleased and impressed. Karl leaves the meeting with a happy client and a new assignment, making an appointment to return in a few days to discuss the tax issue.

1.4 Customer or client

Lawyers, accountants, advertising agencies and private banks have clients. Commercial banks, restaurants and retail outlets have customers. What's in a label? Well, quite a lot it turns out.

Turn to any dictionary and a 'customer' is typically defined as a person who buys goods [or commodities] or services. The definition is simple and describes a simple transactional relationship. The use of the word 'commodities' in some definitions further hints at the non-committal status of the relationship between vendor and purchaser.

The word 'client' on the other hand is defined in its simplest form as a person using the services of a professional person or organisation and in fuller versions as a person that depends on the protection of another. The word 'client' in fact derives from the latin word *cliens* denoting a person under the protection and patronage of another. The word client implies a 'duty of care' and suggests a longer-term relationship.

In a commercial setting, businesses with customers tend to have transactional relationships, where loyalty is low, and the purchasing decision is based on tangible features (e.g. interest rates, product specifications) and price. Businesses with clients often offer less-tangible products and services (e.g. ideas, quality advice, personal service) and a purchasing decision where price is a factor, but not the prime factor.

Perhaps it is no surprise then to find major commercial banks, who want to build deeper relationships with their corporate customers, increasingly refer to 'clients' in their promotional literature. Unfortunately, however, operational change is harder to implement than promotional words. This can be reflected in a mismatch between the words in promotional materials and the behaviour of sales and customer service professionals, who constantly promote new financial products that may be completely unsuited to individual customers.

Organisations moving from a 'push' method of selling to an approach that caters to the specific needs of individuals – and recognise that they have responsibilities to those individuals – must re-engineer much more than their marketing literature. Operational, financial and human resource systems must all be re-aligned.

For example, marketing activities and the behaviour of pre-sales staff can easily be undermined by post-sales activities, if the level of attention pre- and post-sale is not consistent.

For any organisation looking to build deeper, stronger relationships with buyers, an understanding of the sense of responsibility that lawyers and accountants feel towards their clients can yield interesting insights:

■ The service offering is personalised. Time is invested to understand the client's background and needs. This is typically not charged for. Note that personalised service is different to personal service. Some banks, for example, allocated a 'Personal Relationship Manager' to more wealthy account holders, but these people typically have no understanding of customers' needs and continue to offer generic products. Customers quickly realise that this is simply another attempt by the bank to sell more of its products.

■ The relationship manager stays the course, facilitating both the sales and service delivery process, right through the settlement of fees. Contrast this with other organisations where the interest of the salesperson disappears once the sales process is concluded, with responsibility for fulfilment being passed to other departments.

Staying the course has other benefits too. It means that the salesperson is still around to manage the client relationship when, as often happens, the organisation fails to fulfil the salesperson's promises to the client. While it may cause temporary pain for the salesperson to have to deal with an unhappy client, this is generally preferable to leaving someone else to deal with the problem who has a far less developed understanding (and less sensitivity).

Indeed, for the I Owe U practitioner, that moment when something goes wrong is one of the major payback times for the investment they have made in the client relationship. It is well-proven that clients with deep, trusted relationships are much more forgiving of occasional mistakes and unfulfilled promises.

Armed with an understanding of how I Owe U salespeople seek to build long-term trusted relationships, differentiating their offering through the way that they behave, we are ready to take a closer look at how we currently behave and how our behaviours may be interpreted by others. In the next chapter and its related appendices (Appendix 1 and 2) we look at eight key behaviours that affect sales relationships and we give you the opportunity to assess your own behaviours.

Stately Homes – part 2

A few days after her meeting with Mr Leung, Emily attended a meeting at Bay Ceramics with FuturePerfect's Regional Sales Director, Marilyn Shah.

On the way to the meeting, Marilyn took a detour and stopped off at another former customer to leave some extra copies of user manuals for a system that had been installed the previous year. Emily thought it interesting that Marilyn had not just put the manuals in the post.

When they finally arrived at Bay Ceramics, Emily was feeling impatient. She had a busy day ahead of her and Marilyn seemed to be wasting valuable time.

Emily's impatience increased when Marilyn started the meeting with Bill Tern by talking about how the ceramics industry had been affected by the recent new legislation prohibiting the import of goods from countries where child labour was used in production. Emily could not see how this had anything to do with FuturePerfect. After all, they sold computer systems.

Bill Tern spent ten minutes talking about child labour and Marilyn even encouraged him by talking about the children she had seen working in fireworks factories on a recent visit she had made to India.

Finally, the conversation turned to the subject of FuturePerfect's inventory control and Marilyn explained why she had asked to see him. But, instead of telling him about FuturePerfect's system, she asked him if there was anything else he wanted to talk about. Luckily, thought Emily, he didn't.

Next, when Bill actually asked Marilyn to tell him about Apostle, she declined and said, 'Before I talk about Apostle, I'd really like to get a better sense of how you organise your inventory, and how inventory management impacts other aspects of your business.'

Bill talked for a further half-hour, and all Marilyn seemed to do was relate stories of where she had seen other companies have similar issues. She didn't talk about Apostle at all. Then, abruptly, Bill looked at his watch and said they would need to end the meeting there.

Marilyn did a quick verbal summary then ended by saying they would go away, think about what Bill had said, and see if FuturePerfect could help in any way.

Emily thought nothing more of the meeting until three months later when she heard that Bay had just engaged FuturePerfect to co-ordinate the development of a new enterprise-wide inventory management system for all their offices around the globe. It was the largest project of the year for FuturePerfect.

Perhaps, thought Emily, her impatience was not justified.

Key messages

- ■ Too many buyer–seller relationships are deficient in trust, enjoyment and shared commitment.

- ■ 'Push' sales methods are increasingly counter-productive since every buyer and every conversation is unique. Prescriptive approaches will not work.

- ■ Consultative sales approaches focus more on buyers' needs, but can also be manipulative – targeting areas of interest to sellers rather than buyers.

- ■ I Owe U is a next-generation consultative approach that takes the buyer on a more natural and engaging sales journey – differentiating the seller from the competition.

- In conversations, control rests with the buyer, with the salesperson following the thoughts of the buyer.

- The salesperson must recognise that they have a responsibility to the buyer that goes beyond securing the current sale.

2

How other people really see you

'It is often tragic to see how blatantly a man bungles his own life and the lives of others yet remains totally incapable of seeing how much the whole tragedy originates in himself, and how he continually feeds it and keeps it going.'

> Carl Jung (1875–1961), Founder of analytical psychology

I Owe U demands honesty, and that honesty begins with developing a deeper understanding of your own behaviours and how those behaviours affect buyers. This chapter focuses on developing that understanding.

Arc Inc – part 1

Richard and Emily had recently been engaging their customers in more business discussions and were being less 'pushy' in their selling, despite the increased sales targets. They had certainly seen an improvement in the way that most customers seemed to treat them and there had been an increase in sales.

However, in the past few months they had found it increasingly hard to sell their product against the competition.

They thought that the market's perception of their product had changed and that maybe their main competitor's product was now seen as better by their buyers. Richard and Emily knew this was not the case and they worked very hard to persuade their buyers accordingly.

Arc Inc had been given good feedback about FuturePerfect by

▶

contacts and had therefore given Richard and Emily the chance to propose for their work.

Arc Inc had never bought anything in the area of back office integrated software before. There was therefore an element of education needed in the sales process.

Emily talked a lot about the huge savings that Arc Inc would make if they used FuturePerfect's Apostle system. They believed this argument should help Arc Inc see past the fact that their product was marginally more expensive than competing products.

They demonstrated their product to Mr Jones, the key buyer, and showed how it made a big difference to other companies. They thought this was a very good opportunity for Arc Inc.

Every company that has previously taken a chance on this product has been delighted by the results – so Arc Inc should also take the plunge.

The meeting with Arc Inc felt good for Emily and Richard. They brainstormed and came up with new ideas for additional functionality that could be added to the standard Apostle system to deliver a superior product for Arc Inc.

Unfortunately, several weeks later Mr Jones rang to say that Arc Inc had decided not to buy the product.

2.1 Why you need to know how others see you

We have worked with dozens of organisations and thousands of individuals who sell products or services. But, what they really sell is themselves. Most markets are now so competitive, with buyers facing ever greater choice, that products and services can no longer be easily distinguished and where buyers used to see specialised offerings, they now see a commodity.

Faced with this challenge, salespeople have two choices. They can differentiate themselves on price (the easy route for the salesperson and the one most followed – but one that leads to lower profits for the vendor), or differentiate based on how the product or service is provided. The second route is much harder, and more challenging. It requires the salesperson to stay involved with the buyer way beyond the initial sale, and it also involves personal risk.

The personal risk is present because the buyer's decision to purchase becomes a decision principally based on their feelings about the salesperson.

Over the years we have conducted hundreds of buyer feedback interviews on behalf of our clients. It never ceases to surprise us how the feedback from a buyer differs from the perception that the seller had about their relationship.

In this chapter and the accompanying appendices – Appendix 1 and 2 – we will help you recognise the different ways in which people behave and the impact that has on other people. We also give you the opportunity to 'measure' your own behaviour. You will then be able to compare your behaviours with those of an effective I Owe U salesperson and put in place action plans to help you make any shifts in your behaviour that you want.

This process will also help to put many of the messages covered in this book into a personal perspective and will help you apply the associated skills more effectively.

2.2 Who you are

You are born with what A H Almass calls 'essence' (in his book *The Pearl Beyond Price* (2000)). A combination of that 'essence' and your upbringing in your formative years determines your personality. Your personality, coupled with your broadening experience of the world around you (and the impact of the actions you take), in turn establishes your behaviour patterns (see Figure 2.1).

We all have our preferred ways of behaving, and the actions we take are expressions of our preferred behaviours. A distinction does need to be drawn though between our immediate behaviours and our overall behaviour patterns. Broad patterns of behaviour are formed over time and are difficult to change, whereas immediate behaviours can be changed instantly – to help us achieve a particular outcome, or because we see that the impact of our preferred behaviour patterns is not what we desired.

We are not suggesting that people can or should change their personalities in order to build better business relationships. What we are suggesting is

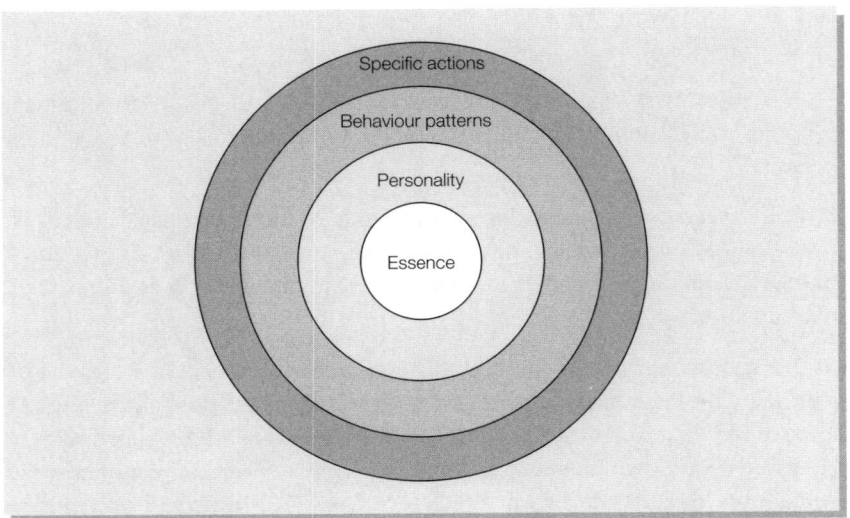

figure 2.1   **What makes up you**

that you can decide to change specific actions instantly. You can even 'flick the switch' and make changes to your behaviour that are not in accordance with your personality, but such behaviour takes effort and is hard to maintain. A common example of this would be sharing in the social activities of a buyer, despite the fact that you are quiet and introvert in nature. You might learn to be more extrovert in this buyer's company, but it would be hard work.

The remainder of this chapter helps you to understand how you tend to behave and how your behaviour may be interpreted by others. Ideally, after completing the self-assessment in Appendix 1 or by referring to any previous assessment you may have taken, you should also ask your colleagues to complete an assessment on you. This feedback (typically referred to as 360-degree feedback) is often very revealing, since we tend not to see ourselves as others see us. Within the confines of this book we clearly cannot do the 360, however we do suggest you consider this as an option at some stage.

A word of warning. Smart people do not always have a natural desire to learn and change. Edward de Bono and Chris Almass, to name but two management gurus and thinkers, would argue that to a certain extent the more intellectually smart you are, the less likely you are to accept readily that you are in fact not perfect and can improve.

The problem is that you are, almost by definition, successful. You got to be successful by doing what you do. So why would you want to change? In fact, is there not a risk that in changing you may become less successful?

If you are changing because someone else tells you to change then you may change behaviour in some given instances, but there is a good chance that your body will send signals that suggest this behaviour is a pretence, and the people around you will quickly realise that your behaviour is a sham. Also, if you have not bought in to the change, and sometimes even when you have, there is a good chance that you will revert to your old behaviour type pretty quickly when under stress.

2.3 The Octagon™ Behavioural Assessment

As we mentioned above there are two steps to the awareness stage of a development process. The first is self-awareness, where you get a sense of whether the tool you are using gives you the results you expect from answering questions about yourself.

The second is where you get feedback from others on how they see you: the 360-degree assessment. In this book we only facilitate the self-assessment. We do however give some information at the end of this chapter about the 360-degree process.

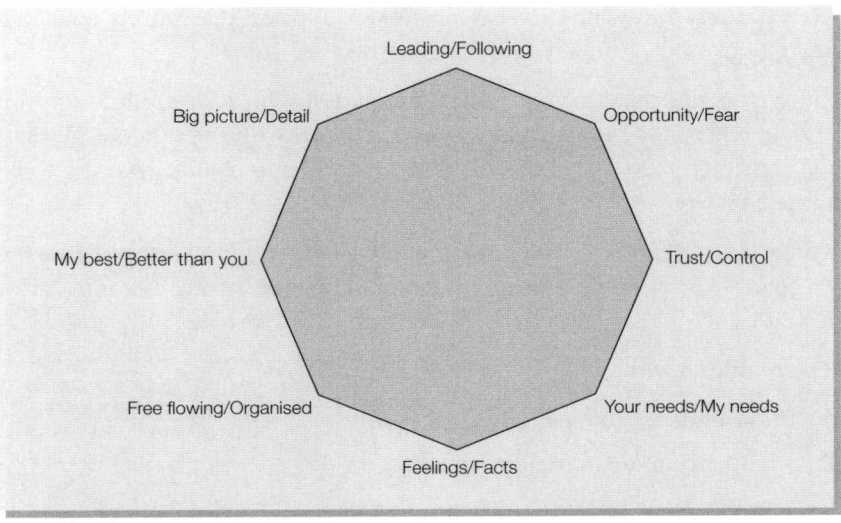

figure 2.2 The eight Octagon™ behaviour categories

Over the next few pages you will measure your own behaviour. The tool you will use is the Octagon™. This is a straightforward tool, developed with the assistance of a panel of psychologists.

The Octagon™ measures eight behaviours, each with two extremes (see Figure 2.2). There is no right or wrong, just an understanding of how you behave, and how that translates into how others perceive you.

As we will discuss in Chapters 4 and 5, building rapport is one of the keys to effective relationship building and selling. One of the most effective ways to build rapport is to match the behaviours of the buyer. In order to be able to do that, it helps to understand how you naturally behave in all eight categories shown in Figure 2.2.

There are, however, three categories that are specifically linked to being a powerful I Owe U salesperson. Generally speaking, a great I Owe U salesperson will score highly in Trust, Your needs and Feelings.

In Appendix 1, you can generate your personal Octagon™ behavioural profile by first answering a series of questions; then scoring your individual answers; and finally by sketching your profile. The whole process should take between 20 and 40 minutes.

The Octagon™ profile and sales behaviours

The accuracy of your self-score in any assessment will be determined by your honesty and your self-awareness. We will proceed assuming your self-score results do accurately reflect how others see you.

Once you understand your behaviour patterns in a sales situation you should reflect and decide whether you are happy with the results and if not decide which of your behaviours you would like to change in order to be more effective.

There is no definitive shape for a good I Owe U salesperson. However, in Figure 2.3 we show a shape that would suggest strong alignment to I Owe U.

The profile shown in Figure 2.3 suggests:

1   the confidence to *lead*, when necessary

2   a tendency to embrace *opportunities*

3   a strong desire to *trust* a person or process

4   a strong preference for focusing on the *needs of others*

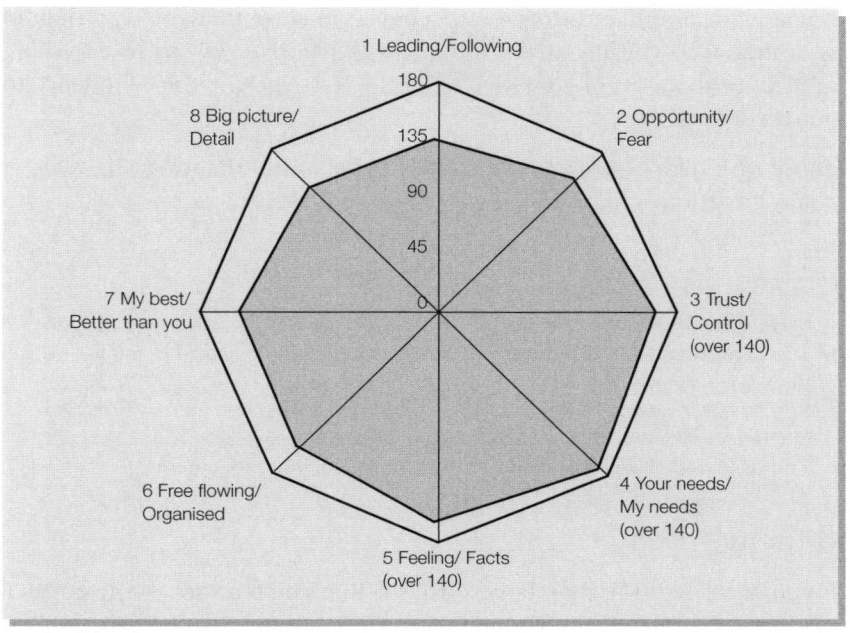

figure 2.3 The I Owe U behaviour profile

5 a strong sensitivity to *feelings* and social atmospheres

6 a tendency to allow things to *freely* find their own course

7 a desire to be the *best* you can be

8 a preference for dealing with the *bigger picture*.

Let's now take a closer look at how each behaviour affects the way you sell.

Below we summarise the typical behaviours associated with each score, in the broad context of a sales relationship and the specific, critical context of face-to-face meetings. There is a far more detailed explanation of each behaviour in Appendix 2. That appendix also includes a planning document to help you decide what you are going to do in the future to try to change.

Leading / Following

If you score over 140 then the buyer will notice that you tend to be the first to say things. You might be perceived by some buyers as too directive. You may be seen by buyers as not listening enough to them.

If you score around or below 40 then buyers may see that you tend only to say things if specifically asked. You might be perceived by buyers as lacking in ideas or thoughts of your own or, at the least, lacking the confidence to put them forward.

Those with high or low scores are likely to behave in the following ways in a sales situation:

Leading (high score)	Following (low score)
▦ You will ask the buyer questions	▦ You will answer the buyer's questions
▦ You start the conversation with the buyer	▦ You wait for the buyer to come to you or to talk to you first
▦ You fill every silence in a conversation with the buyer	▦ You leave silence for the buyer to fill in during conversations
▦ You make definitive statements	▦ You caveat your statements

Opportunity / Fear

If you score over 140 then buyers will see that you tend to see the positive in things. You may however be perceived by a buyer as someone who is unrealistic, maybe a little reckless and too prepared to try things that have not been well thought through.

If you score around or below 40 then the buyer will see that you tend to be concerned about the risks of new ideas. You may be perceived by a buyer as someone who spends a lot of time talking about the problems and dangers of an idea rather than the potential upside of resolving the issue.

Those with high or low scores are likely to behave in the following ways in a sales situation:

Opportunity (high score)	Fear (low score)
▦ You ask questions about opportunities for the buyer's business	▦ You ask questions about threats to the buyer's business
▦ You explain how much the purchase will help the buyer	▦ You point out the problems of the purchase to the buyer
▦ You try to 'enthuse' the buyer into purchasing	▦ You try to 'frighten' the buyer into purchasing

Trust / Control

If you score over 140 then buyers will see that you naturally tend to trust people. You may however be perceived by buyers as too hands-off, even disinterested.

If you score around or below 40 then buyers will feel that you tend to stay in control. You may be viewed by buyers as driving conversations and the relationship and not listening and letting them do the driving.

Those with high or low scores are likely to behave in the following ways in a sales situation:

Trust (high score)	Control (low score)
■ You ask open questions and let the buyer dictate the conversation	■ You ask closed questions to direct the conversation
■ You let the buyer control the pace and timing of a purchase	■ You tell the buyer what they should buy
■ You are happy to pass buyers to colleagues because you know they would do the same for you	■ Once you think you have a sale you will try to close quickly

Your needs / My needs

If you score over 140 then buyers will feel that you are trying to help them – even at your own expense. However, whilst seeing you as helpful, some buyers may see you as not being as self-confident as you could be.

If you score around or below 40 then buyers will feel that you tend to do things only if there is something in it for you. Buyers may perceive selfish motives in your actions and feel that you do not listen to their needs sufficiently.

Those with high or low scores are likely to behave in the following ways in a sales situation:

Your needs (high score)	My needs (low score)
■ You ask the buyer what they want	■ You say things such as 'You need to understand . . .'
■ You challenge the buyer to buy something that may be more appropriate for them – even if it may be a smaller sale	■ You push the buyer towards purchasing something that helps your sales figures
	■ You will take a quick sale and then move on to the next potential buyer
■ You try to understand more about the buyer's needs to see if there are any other value-add items they would benefit from	■ You try to on-sell additional items regardless of whether they add value to the buyer

Feelings / Facts

If you score over 140 then buyers will see you as being fair. Some buyers may however see you as too 'touchy-feely' and more concerned with the well-being of people than on making money.

If you score around or below 40 then you may not be able to engage well with buyers. You may be perceived by some buyers as cold, unfeeling and inconsiderate of others.

Those with high or low scores are likely to behave in the following ways in a sales situation:

Feelings (high score)	Facts (low score)
■ You ask the buyer about their personal needs and goals	■ You ask the buyer about their business needs
■ You talk about how the purchase will help the buyer and the people they work closely with	■ You talk to the buyer about how the purchase will help the buyer's organisation
■ You talk to the buyer about your own personal situation	■ You talk about the cost and efficiency of the purchase
■ You will engage with all the buyer's team members	■ You talk to the buyer about your role as a salesperson
■ You will be able to relate to many different types of buyer	■ You focus on dealing with the economic buyer in any given situation
	■ You may find it a challenge to deal with buyers who are not similar to you

Free flowing / Organised

If you score over 140 then buyers will see that you are prepared to go with the flow. Some buyers may also see you as somewhat disorganised.

If you score around or below 40 then buyers will see that you like to plan things out well in advance. The danger here is that buyers may see you as being too focused on the plan with a tendency to lose sight of the objectives. They may also believe that you are not adaptable enough to changing circumstances.

Those with high or low scores are likely to behave in the following ways in a sales situation:

Free flowing (high score)	Organised (low score)
■ You will have no plan of action for a buyer, you will take things as they come ■ You will be happy with just having objectives for a meeting with a buyer and see no need for a detailed agenda ■ You will find yourself having last minute 'panics' to meet buyer deadlines	■ You have a more or less standard script for sales ■ You will have agendas for buyer meetings ■ You will bring the conversation back on track if it strays from your agenda ■ You will have a very organised plan of action for a potential buyer

My best / Better than you

If you score over 140 then buyers will see that you are driven to achieve the best result possible. Some buyers may however feel that you are self-centred and too focused.

If you score around or below 40 then buyers will see you are driven by making sure that no-one else will achieve better results. You may be seen as worrying too much about beating the competition, rather than focusing on achieving the best possible result.

Persons with high or low scores are likely to behave in the following ways in a sales situation:

My best (high score)	Better than you (low score)
■ You will do whatever you can to be the best salesperson there is ■ You will work as hard as you can to help buyers or sell to them ■ You assume you will achieve your sales target	■ You will focus on being the best salesperson in the team or on achieving your sales target ■ You may try to 'show off' to a buyer by showing how much you know about the product ■ You may deal with buyers even though someone else in your organisation may be a better match for that buyer in order to help your sales figures

Big picture / Detail

If you score over 140 then buyers will see that you can engage with their strategy and vision. You may be seen by some buyers as someone who does not pay enough attention to the details.

If you score around or below 40 then buyers will see that you understand the details and reality of the situation. Some buyers may feel you have a tendency to get bogged down in the detail.

Those with high or low scores are likely to behave in the following ways in a sales situation:

Big picture (high score)	Detail (low score)
■ You will ask the buyer what they are trying to achieve with this purchase ■ You will sell the impact of your offering to the buyer ■ You will link your offering to the buyer's strategy and vision ■ You will talk about the long-term advantages of the purchase	■ You will ask the buyer about current problems ■ You will sell the detail of how your offering will work for the buyer ■ You will link your offering to the buyer's current problems ■ You talk about the immediate advantages of buying the purchase

2.4 What are you going to do next?

Having taken the Octagon™ assessment you now have a better idea of the sorts of behaviour that you demonstrate in given situations and the potential impact it can have on buyers.

How do your scores compare to those above? What does this mean for the way you are perceived by buyers? These are the really important questions.

If you are comfortable with your results then there is no need to do anything further.

If however you are uncomfortable with the results and how they affect your ability to sell then you can start planning actions. You can either do this on your own or you might consider obtaining some help from an expert in the area of behaviour and communication.

If there are a few people in the organisation reading this book at the same time then consider discussing your results in a group session. This can be a very powerful way to start breaking down individuals' reluctance to change. Seeing that others have similar profiles and face similar challenges tends to be reassuring. As a result, people start to talk about things they have never mentioned before.

If you would like to develop your own action plan then go to Appendix 2 where we have included an action plan for you to complete. If you would like a full-sized copy of that plan then download it for free from www.ioweu.com.

2.5 Finding out what other people really think

Once your self-assessment is complete, you may want to consider a full 360-degree review – to find out how others see you.

There are two common approaches to this. Anonymous feedback or one where the person requesting the feedback chooses who provides the feedback. We advocate the latter because:

■ It reduces defensive reactions when the results come in.

■ It creates better buy-in to changing behaviours because people have chosen those whose opinions they value.

■ It gives you an opportunity to seek ongoing coaching from these individuals during and after the process.

For meaningful results, between five and 10 people should be chosen, with differing relationships to the person requesting the feedback. These people should be asked in advance if they are willing to participate – preferably by the person who wants the feedback. This helps them feel more comfortable and encourages honesty.

You may decide to work out what to do with the feedback on your own, but we would recommend receiving the feedback one-on-one with a professional facilitator/coach. As we mentioned earlier, unexpected feedback is quite common and it helps to have a facilitator/coach present to manage the reaction. Understanding how your behaviours are interpreted by others is the first step to becoming a more complete I Owe U salesperson.

In the next chapter we change focus and look at the different types of relationships that typically exist between buyers and sellers. We outline four common relationship types then introduce strategies for moving relationships from one type to another.

Arc Inc – part 2

Having taken the Octagon™, Emily scored 120 on Opportunity, 110 on Free flowing and 130 on Big picture. Very proud of the scores, she looked at what that meant and also looked at the workbook.

The Octagon™ suggested that someone with Emily's scores may come across as:

- happy to get involved with new ideas, sometimes regardless of risk
- not very good at methodical planning
- impatient when it comes to talking about detail

Arc Inc, to whom they were trying to sell their product, had recently been in a court case where they had made some significant errors of judgement. The key buyer, Mr Jones, is a lawyer by background.

Emily decided there was a high likelihood that Mr Jones is risk averse and keen on looking into every detail before making a decision. It might be that he had seen Emily as a rather maverick person more interested in what the software could do rather than if the software would work properly.

Emily called Mr Jones to talk through:

- a recent detailed implementation plan and post-implementation review that had been applied at a similar-sized organisation in a related industry
- a detailed risk and reward matrix for every stage of Arc Inc's proposed implementation.

Mr Jones did not change his mind and decide to buy from her rather than her competitor, but he did say that Arc Inc would be very interested in looking at the documentation that Emily had put together.

Key messages

■ Self understanding – of your behavioural preferences, and how these impact others – is the starting point for building better relationships.

■ You cannot decide to change your personality, but you can decide to change your outward behaviour – if you so choose.

■ The way that you behave determines the way that others behave towards you.

■ Behaviours must be genuine. False behaviours are quickly seen for what they are.

■ There is a strong positive correlation between high Octagon™ scores and I Owe U sales success – especially in Trust, Your needs and Feelings.

3

Understanding and changing your relationships

'Treasure your relationships not your possessions.'

Anthony J D'Angelo

I Owe U salespeople focus on the quality of relationship they have at any given time with their buyer rather than on the sales they have made to that buyer. In this chapter we will look at how you can measure the relationship you have with your buyer and how you can change it into a more trusting and deeper one.

YarrA Limited – part 1

Richard and Emily recently had a meeting with the CFO, Rebecca, and Purchasing Manager, Kiran, of YarrA Limited to talk about systems integration. They have good relationships with both Rebecca and Kiran. Richard has been to the football several times with Kiran and they always have a lot of fun. At her previous employer Rebecca bought systems from Emily.

Emily let the meeting follow a natural course rather than try to dictate the pace and content. It started really well with Richard and Kiran reflecting back on some fun evenings at the football. Rebecca then outlined why systems integration was becoming more important for YarrA. She also said that she was very busy and that she needed to keep the meeting short and focused. At the end of her explanation, Rebecca asked if Richard and Emily would submit a proposal including a definitive price.

▶

Richard and Emily were initially very happy about the meeting and the fact that they were asked to propose. Systems integration consulting was a new and growing revenue stream for FuturePerfect and it would be good to land this project.

However, they started to get concerned about pricing as they looked more closely at Rebecca's requirements. They tried calling her several times over the following week, but she was always busy. They did speak to Kiran and he said that the more detail they could give Rebecca, the better. She likes to understand how prices are calculated.

They submitted their proposal on time and were confident that, because of their history with Kiran and Rebecca, they would win the work. A few days passed and they received a letter advising them that they had not been successful. A rather despondent Richard called Kiran – who told them that their price was too high.

3.1 Types of relationship

Many salespeople tell us, when we first meet them, that they have excellent relationships with their buyers – or at least with some of them. Often however, when we dig a little deeper, we find that the relationships are built on shallow foundations.

To build and maintain deep and successful relationships, the first step is to understand your buyer's view: after all, the quality of a relationship is defined by the way the buyer feels about it – not you. With an improved understanding you will be better able to:

■ ensure that you have the right number of buyers in each category to minimise risk and maximise opportunities for short- and long-term success

■ plan your overall strategy for each buyer in a more effective manner

■ decide on what to say and ask at the next interaction with a specific buyer in order to advance the relationship.

We have identified four different types of relationships you can have with your buyers. We describe business relationships in terms of primarily social, ad-hoc, technical or partner (see Figure 3.1).

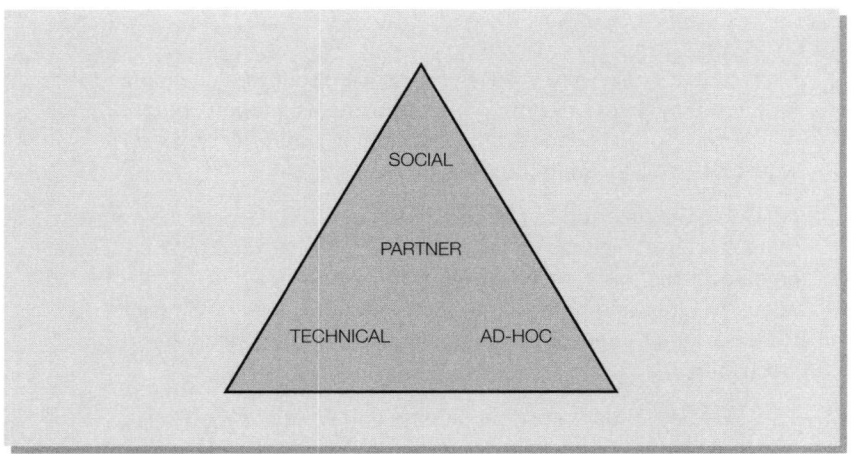

figure 3.1   **Four business relationships**

A partnering, collaborative relationship sits at the centre of the I Owe U salesperson's universe and is always our target – when we feel that this is also the right relationship for the buyer (see Chapter 4). The partnership relationship is where most benefit is to be gained for both the buyer and the seller.

Whilst the labels attached to each type of relationship are not so important, we will see that there are different and significant implications for the salesperson attaching to each relationship type.

The remainder of this chapter deals with the characteristics of each relationship type and the steps that can be taken to move relationships towards the centre.

Social relationships

Characteristics

These relationships often start through a chance social meeting that subsequently takes on a business aspect. Alternatively, they can start with the suggestion of a casual meeting at a coffee shop, over lunch or after work – then fail to make the transition to a full business relationship.

In such relationships you like the buyer and you share some common interests. You may get some work from these relationships, but generally small pieces of work and not that frequently. Conversation is primarily social and generally quite superficial. The location for the conversations is often a fairly public setting not suited to an in-depth business discussion. Whilst the buyer usually accepts the invitations it is normally you initiating the event. The seller controls the relationship.

Aaron and Bill: a social relationship that's stuck in a rut

The seller's (Aaron's) perspective:
'Bill's one of the good guys. He's a lively, amiable person holding a senior regional position at a multinational financial services company. We've known each other for years. We used to share a taxi or bus to work when we lived in the same area.

'We meet every so often, always at my initiation, and usually after a few postponements. Usually Bill suggests we meet for lunch, drinks or dinner. We talk about family, our mutual interest in property investment and our dreams for retirement.

'I've done work for Bill in the past, but not recently. He asks for my help sometimes, but typically at very short notice. I've had to turn him down because of other commitments.

'What frustrates me these days is that Bill always talks about the big plans that his company has and how he sees that I can help, but the projects never materialise.'

The buyer's (Bill's) perspective:
'I like Aaron. He's a friendly person and I trust him. I generally enjoy our meetings but I feel a bit guilty that we haven't given him any work recently. We've involved Aaron in a few projects historically and they went fine. I've also introduced him to other people in the business and I think that led to work.

'I do need to be careful that I'm not perceived as giving work to my friends.

'Meetings with Aaron can be a bit tricky these days. We talk about family and plans for the future, but dance around any discussion about work. Consequently, if a pressing business issue comes up, I tend to postpone the meetings. I feel bad, but I only have so much time to spare.'

Advantages of this type of relationship

This relationship is fun for you and for the buyer. It is easy and, if anything, is an escape from the business element of your work. You may even see it as reward for all the hard work you put in.

You may also be providing the buyer with something he cannot get elsewhere, such as tickets to a popular event, and they may be grateful for that.

Disadvantages of this type of relationship

There is little or no business buy-in and it is easy for someone to take your place by simply being more sociable. The relationship can also soak up a lot of personal time, in addition to work time. Taken to extremes, social relationships can border on bribery – a very dangerous place to be.

In normal circumstances there is also a risk that the buyer may become inundated with social relationship offers. Research shows that the higher a buyer gets in an organisation the more a seller wants to 'entertain' them. Thus these buyers tend to receive multiple entertainment offers and as a result value them less. Many organisations invest heavily in entertaining for little real improvement in the relationship.

Where work is given there is sometimes an expectation of discounts. You may feel pressure to do a better job than for other buyers because you would hate to upset your 'friend'. You may even do the job on a loss basis because you found it hard to turn the offer down. This can have disadvantages for the buyer's organisation because in doing the buyer a 'favour' proper protocols are often ignored and risks increase.

Ad-hoc relationships

Characteristics

There is some work, and it can be big projects, but the work is not constant or consistent. It is reactive and urgent. They buy your ability to sort out a mess. They do not see you as a key provider, but as someone who can sort things out when they've run out of other options. The buyer controls the relationship.

The seller sees the work as a distinct project with a start – signing the contract – and an end – issuing the fee.

Marie the managament consultant: an ad-hoc relationship heading for no-hoc!

The seller's (Marie's) perspective:

'We are their preferred supplier. They are a large mining company and every time they have a problem they call us to help them out. They are big projects with big revenues and good profits. Stressful, but we make them pay for our stress!

'Three years ago they needed to buy the partner out of one of their joint ventures. They called us to provide advice. We pulled together a focused and succinct proposal and we won the work. They were happy with what we did and paid the fee without dispute.

'Then last year, they were looking to bring in a new business partner and again they called and asked us to propose to manage the business integration process. The proposal process did take a bit longer that time though as they pressed us harder to justify our fee. Still, we won in the end and it turned out to be a big project. Again the client paid the fee without question.

'I'm sure that next time they need help in this area they will call us.'

The buyer's perspective:

'They are very good at what they do – advising on large transactions. Their prices are increasingly on the high side, but we can usually get them down to a number we are happy with. If we could not then we would go to someone else.

'We don't hear from them between projects and the onus is always on us to call them when we have a need. I guess that's OK, but it does mean that we have to educate them each time on what has happened since we were last in contact. Because they are doing lots of deal-connected work all the time, we also wonder sometimes if they might have other knowledge, or come across opportunities, that we don't get to hear about, because they don't stay close to us.

'The good news though is that because we don't have a strong relationship we can squeeze them on price, with no huge downside if we end up pushing them too far. They are good, but so are a number of their competitors. So we push until we get a price we are happy with.

'There is another provider around who genuinely seems interested in us and they call us several times a year to find out what is happening

> in our business. Next time we have a need, we will still have to use
> our standard tender process, but if this other provider is close on
> price and has the right capabilities, we'll give them a try.'

Advantages of this type of relationship

You need to put in little effort on an ongoing basis. It is a very pleasant surprise when the business comes because it has not been budgeted for. Potentially there are large revenue gains to be made.

Disadvantages of this type of relationship

There is no buyer loyalty. You often need to go through a proposal process to secure specific pieces of business and price can be a big issue. Typically projects are urgent and can put huge stress on your people. You don't get to know the ongoing strategy for their business or identify future needs. The relationship may not be with a key buyer. You cannot plan budgets or resources for the work.

There is a risk of a low profit, even with large revenue, if there is an onerous proposal process or the buyer squeezes the price.

Technical relationships

Characteristics

This is generally a reactive relationship where the buyer purchases knowledge, expertise or quality of product. There can be a steady flow of business, but there is no deep connection on a personal level. Indeed, buyers may find that talking to you is difficult or boring since you only ever talk about business.

Whilst the buyer values the fact that you 'know your stuff', at the extreme your deeper technical expertise may cause them discomfort. Experts often have the knack of making lesser mortals feel rather inferior!

Buyers sometimes see you as one of a series of options and they control the relationship.

Francis the web-designer: a technical relationship that died

The seller's (Francis's) perspective:
'We've got a good relationship with Adam and his team. They run a travel booking web site and we've custom-built their site to cross-link information from multiple sources. It's quite challenging technically and it stretched our system to its limit.

'Six months after the site was built, they wanted major changes to the look and feel. This involved changing a large number of custom page-frames. Really quite time-consuming. We gave them a good price to do it though.

'Next, they decided to add a forum. Again, we responded well. We were able to find a low-cost web forum template and plug it into their site. They were up and running pretty quickly.

'Most recently, they've talked to us about building sister sites, so I guess we must be doing OK. The only thing I would say is that they do complain about costs quite a lot, but I have told them that they could save some money by learning some basic HTML so they can do some of the maintenance themselves.'

The buyer's (Adam's) perspective:
'I didn't really like Francis the first time I met him, but my boss had already made the decision. He came across as a bit too confident – a bit of a know-it-all. To hear him talk you would think that running a web-based business was very easy.

'Although the system achieved 90% of what we needed, it wasn't easy to get their attention when we wanted updates. Over time the only common contact from Francis was the monthly invoice for hosting the site.

'We then came across another potential web hosting service in Hong Kong that was cheaper. Subsequently we decided to change service provider, not because of price, but because the Hong Kong company seemed more interested in us and offered a number of ideas about different directions we could take the web site.'

Advantages of this type of relationship

Assuming that you have a technically good offering, and you know it well, then the relationship is easy for you. You feel comfortable talking in detail about your offering and answering any questions. It is a relatively quick relationship to build – especially if your company's brand gives the buyer confidence.

Disadvantages of this type of relationship

Unless you have a clear technical advantage over competitors then price can be the main differentiator. You are likely to have to re-propose frequently, since limited loyalty exists. Your offering is seen as a commodity.

It is relatively easy for a competitor to displace you (a) if they take the time to better understand the buyer and the business relationship and (b) with a lower price (where they can match the technical aspects of your offering).

Finally, the buyer will tend not to forgive mistakes.

Partner relationships

Characteristics

This is the most advantageous relationship for both the salesperson and the buyer. Whatever the buyer thinks you can do, they ask you to do. You also get asked to help in areas outside your expertise – because they value your thoughts, ideas and contacts even though you may not have the answer to a particular issue or question.

This is a personal, strategic relationship. They buy you. They trust you to help them. They trust you to tell them who is the best provider of any service or product. They do not make decisions without your input. It is a peer relationship. You both get equal value out of the relationship. You are happy to refer other people to your buyer, either from within or outside your organisation as your relationship is strong enough for you not to worry about any risks associated with such a referral.

The relationship is driven by both the buyer and the seller.

Allan Chu the builder: a partner for life?

The seller's (Allan's) perspective:
'I like Peter – he's a good guy. He bought a flat in Hong Kong that I was renovating for a family friend. The friend had paid me to do a Chinese-style renovation and sell it. Peter asked me to change it to

▶

Western-style. I'd only done the kitchen so far, so it wasn't hard to change.

'He told me what he wanted and I helped him find it. We used to jump in a taxi and go together to the building store. He would pick what he liked, then I would negotiate the price and fit it for him. Some things he bought himself. He should have let me get them for him as he paid too much.

'Once the flat was ready, he said he wanted to invest in Hong Kong flats. So now he buys the flats, I renovate them and we split the profits.

'We meet up for drinks too, maybe twice a month. That helps to keep the fun in the relationship.'

The buyer's (Peter's) perspective:
'Allan Chu's a good guy. It is not easy buying a flat as a foreigner in Hong Kong. These guys are traders and they look at every deal in isolation. If someone can take advantage of you because you don't know the rules of the game, they will.

'Allan was different. He seemed to want to help. He made things very easy for me – smoothing the path whenever he could. He did good work, the way I wanted it. Plus he's a fun guy – always smiling.

'My wife has a problem with him though. She says he overcharges. That may be right, but he's always there in an emergency if I need him. Like the time a washer went at 9pm, and water was spraying everywhere one hour before I was due to leave for a two-week overseas trip. He dropped what he was doing and came straight round to my flat to fix it.

'We've also worked on three investment properties together and we've done well out of those. He helped me buy my new car too – he seems to know all the right people to get a good deal!

'I'm also thinking of opening an office in China, and whilst opening offices is not Allan's business, he was the first person I called to talk through the idea. He talked me through some stories he had heard from people who had already done something similar and put me in contact with one of those companies.'

Advantages of this type of relationship

Loyalty and trust. There are few or no missed opportunities. You get involved early, when they are considering decisions. You save time through bypassing normal sales and proposal processes (which becomes a rubber-stamping exercise that needs to happen to satisfy the buyer's own internal processes). Having this relationship at one level with a buyer often makes it easy to move the relationship up the buyer's hierarchy. You get significant referrals. It is a mutually rewarding relationship. The buyer forgives your mistakes. Price is not a differentiator – indeed, it is seldom discussed.

Disadvantages of this type of relationship

It can take time to build and maintain. It takes personal energy. Much of the time and energy you expend is not directly paid for. You need to have skills outside your technical area in order to be able to develop and maintain these relationships.

You need to respect and care about the buyer even though you may not have a natural personality fit.

3.2 Knowing where you are with a relationship

The key to understanding where you are with a relationship is not by thinking about how you (the salesperson) feel about it, but how the buyer feels about it. You can get a sense of how the buyer views the relationship by reflecting on what happens on the occasions when you meet face-to-face:

- Who calls the meetings, you or the buyer?
- Why are the meetings called? If you call the meetings is it because you have something new to sell or just because you would like to catch up? If the buyer calls the meeting is it because they have a need in your area of expertise, they have a need outside your area of expertise, or they just want to catch up?
- What is discussed when you meet? Mostly social stuff? Only topics where you have obvious experience or expertise?
- How does the meeting run? Any long silences? Who does most of the talking?
- Where are the meetings typically held? The office, coffee shop, meeting room, board room, bar, sports event or other social event?

Name of buyer	George Jones
Who called the meeting?	I did
Why did that person call the meeting?	I wanted to tell him about our new software.
Think of five discussion points that you initiated in the meeting	How busy I am. How busy he was. How his current inventory software was performing. How our new software performs. I would love to come and demonstrate the new software for him.
Think of five discussion points that the buyer initiated in the meeting	He was arranging his annual conference. His secretary had just resigned after 15 years. What the price of the new software was.
What was said to wrap up the meeting – by both of you?	He said he would think about it and get back to me. I said I would call him in a week to see if he needed any more information.

figure 3.2   Assessing relationships through face-to-face meetings

To help you reflect, think of a relationship with one of your key buyers and complete the form in Appendix 4 regarding the last meeting you had with this buyer. See Figure 3.2 to get an idea of the sort of information you should be including.

The answers to the questions on the form will indicate the type of relationship you have. In Figure 3.2 we would conclude that the relationship is an ad-hoc one.

By filling in your own form you will be able to assess your own key relationships.

Why did that person call the meeting?

- If a buyer calls a meeting because they have a need for what you offer that is indicative of a technical or ad-hoc relationship. If this is the first call for a long time, then an ad-hoc relationship is more likely.

- If the seller calls a meeting to discuss a new offering that is indicative of a technical relationship, unless this is in response to a known need.

- If the buyer calls the meeting to just 'catch-up on things' that may indicate a partner relationship – provided the discussion gets around to business issues. Without any serious business discussion, a social relationship is the more likely assessment.

- Conversely, a meeting called by the seller to just 'catch-up' may be indicative of an ad-hoc or social relationship. If it is irregular and an exercise in fishing for business, then an ad-hoc relationship is likely. Regular meetings with superficial discussions to 'catch-up' indicate a social relationship.

- A salesperson who calls a meeting in order to find out or get an update on what is happening both personally and professionally in the buyer's life has a partner relationship – but only if the buyer views the relationship in the same way.

What did you say at the meeting?

- Talking only about the weather, the news, sports, the buyer's family, how busy things are at work (but without more detail) points to a purely social relationship.

- Talking mostly about your offerings suggests an ad-hoc or technical relationship.

- If you simply tell the buyer about how good your offering is and how other buyers have found it very useful, then you are in a technical relationship.
- Taking a genuine interest in, and talking about, the buyer and their business suggests a partner relationship.

What did the buyer say at the meeting?

- If the buyer talked about the weather, families, being busy at work and about general news, but never really talked about their own job or challenges in any depth, then you have a social relationship.
- If the buyer asked you about new offerings, then you are either in a technical or partner relationship.
- If the buyer told you about a need he has now then you are most likely in a technical or an ad-hoc relationship.
- If the buyer asked for your input on something outside your core offering then you are moving towards a partner relationship.

3.3 How to change your relationships

Armed with a better understanding of the relationship you currently have, the question is: Do you want to improve that relationship and, if so, how will you do that?

Some of the most effective salespeople we have come across have a simple question they constantly ask themselves:

How do I ensure that every interaction with a buyer improves the relationship?

Let's think about that. What about the last meeting you had with a buyer? Did you have a clear objective for that meeting? What was it? Did it seek to advance the sale or advance the relationship?

Truly effective salespeople set targets for a defined period and then decide where they would like to get to by the end of the next interaction. They measure success by the conversation they have with their buyer – rather than the number of dollars they have made. To help them plan for this they have documents similar to the one overleaf.

Name of buyer			George Jones				
Relationship level							
Now	**In 2 months**	**In 4 months**	**In 6 months**	**In 8 months**	**In 10 months**	**In 12 months**	**Ultimate**
Ad-hoc	Ad-hoc	Technical	Partner				Partner

What will I say and do in each meeting in order to achieve the next shift in the relationship
Next meeting I will go to the meeting and will not mention our product. I will explain that I am there to find out more about his business. I will ask general questions about how business is doing. I will then hone in on any areas of concern he has, regardless of whether they are something I can help with. I will propose no solutions, just recognise the situation and maybe tell some stories about where I have heard similar concerns. I will send him an email immediately confirming what we discussed and mentioning that I will ask around to see if my other contacts have any ideas.
Second meeting I will briefly refresh him on the issues he raised previously and will ask if these are still the key issues. I will then talk him through some other companies I have come across who have similar issues and how I understand they 'solved' the issues. I will ask if he is interested in speaking directly to these companies for a more in-depth discussion.
Third meeting Depends on what the outcome of the first two meetings is, but I may well introduce him to someone I can find who may be able to help with one of the issues he has raised.

For new relationships, if you can build rapport at the first meeting, it is entirely possible to launch a partner relationship immediately. Here's an example:

On the back of a cold call, we once had a meeting with the Chief Operating Officer of an organisation about their training needs.

We asked questions about his training needs, but the responses were fairly general. We dug into the outcomes he was looking for from training and got more specific responses. We asked about his concerns – and got some good answers regarding things that must not happen through the training, such as inconsistencies between programs, lack of industry knowledge, and lack of cultural sensitivity. We then asked what they had already put in place and what they were currently thinking of planning. At that point it became easy to start conversations where their plans did not match their objectives and may in fact create the risks they were trying to avoid.

At no stage had we even discussed our capability or the extent to which we might or might not be able to help them. We were already helping them.

About 45 minutes into the meeting the COO began to smile knowingly.

We had matched his behaviour and had been asking all the right questions. We had also thrown in some challenging ideas.

We had not suggested we could provide the solution, but we had shown we wanted to help him achieve his objectives. He stopped the meeting and said, 'I think the CEO needs to get involved in this discussion – do you mind?' Of course we didn't. The CEO came in and we continued with our process.

After the meeting we continued the dialogue over a 12-month period. They kept on asking for advice and ideas in areas outside our core offering. We kept on contacting them to see how business was going. Eventually the call came in – we need you to help us improve our training.

No proposal was requested. We did not need one as both parties knew each other's needs and capabilities – and trusted each other. The price was agreed through two emails.

Now, while the process was long, the actual time investment over that period was minimal. Certainly far less than it would have been to go through a whole tender and proposal process.

Is this an ad-hoc or a partner relationship?

The key here is trust. Although contact is only periodic, trust has been established and it is easy to pick up the relationship. Conversations are open and information is freely exchanged. Indeed, this is a feature of partner relationships. Just like our oldest friends, it does not matter if we forget to write or call for a long time – when finally we talk again it is just like old times.

Having said all that, it is not always possible to achieve this in one meeting. The key is to know where you are heading with the relationship.

Sometimes it can be harder to move a well-entrenched technical relation-ship to a partner relationship than it is to go straight from stranger to partner status. It often helps to get colleagues to assist you in making this shift. If you are comfortable with the technical relationship and the buyer is used to it, you may benefit from a third party breaking the pattern of behaviour.

Moving a relationship, especially where a pattern has already been estab-lished, can be time-consuming, stressful and mentally tiring. Sometimes, it can also be unsuccessful – despite your best efforts.

It is a fact that successful people tend to have big egos. And why not – they are successful after all. It is also a fact that people with big egos find it very difficult to admit that they are the wrong person to match with a particular buyer. Where the personal chemistry does not match, we often fool our-selves that we can hide our feelings.

We should not be so foolish with ourselves. Our own instincts tell us when other people are trying too hard to be friendly or when their words are insincere. We pick up the subliminal signals that betray a person's true intentions. Can we really believe that our own bodies do not betray us in the same way?

Our advice: get someone else involved. You can keep trying to hide your feelings, but you will not be able to move the relationship forward. Better to be honest with yourself and let someone else have a go.

Alpha Consultants won a global contract to provide a range of services to Solve Retail. These services included payroll, technology support and training.

The contract was won in the US. As an afterthought, the Asia-Pacific businesses were added – some 4,000 people in eight countries.

Hong Kong was Solve Retail's regional HQ and so Alpha's Hong Kong office became responsible for co-ordinating service delivery to Solve Retail Asia (SRA) throughout the region. There were challenges:

■ Training services were a new offering for Alpha.
■ SRA had not been involved in the selection of Alpha as preferred supplier: Alpha had been forced on them by their US parent company.
■ SRA did not view provision of training as a core competency of Alpha. Since Alpha did not understand training and did not understand SRA's business, SRA's regional leaders wondered how Alpha could possibly provide them with quality training services.
■ Sandra, SRA's Head of Learning, was based in Sydney.

The relationship was ad-hoc. Although Alpha was a preferred supplier, SRA had the option of using other suppliers, in locations where Alpha did not have sufficient capability. In SRA's eyes, that was just about everywhere!

The Alpha relationship holder in Hong Kong was a senior executive with no formal training background. He delegated authority to one of his key managers and was happy to keep a safe distance between himself and SRA's Head of Learning, a fiery and straight-talking Australian.

Time passed. The relationship stagnated. Alpha was not getting a fair share of the work available. Alpha's manager found it hard to cope with the main SRA contact. She was under severe stress working as hard as she could to demonstrate Alpha's capability, but making no headway.

To break the cycle, Alpha introduced a new executive to the account. Joe's job was to try and turn things around and ultimately lead the assignment. He looked at the history and quickly understood where the problem lay. Here was an ad-hoc relationship, coloured by Alpha's corporate ego, with no element of social interaction. It was clear that Alpha were struggling to match SRA's demands, but no-one was

▶

prepared to admit it. SRA's contact knew this, but couldn't get anyone at Alpha to admit it. Where there was no honesty, there could be no trust.

How to move the relationship? Joe knew that a partner relationship incorporates both technical and social elements. Neither was in place here. He decided that building confidence in Alpha's technical capability would be difficult to achieve in the short-term, partly because the capability did not yet exist, and partly because SRA's experience to date had been so poor that they would be sceptical about any claims that the capability was in place. He decided to try to focus on building the personal side of the relationship first, and then add in the 'expert' elements over time, as Alpha's capacity increased.

Joe arranged a face-to-face meeting with Sandra, SRA's Head of Learning, and flew to Sydney. As the new boy on the job, he felt able to admit to Alpha's failings and he empathised with SRA's frustrations. He set out steps for improving the service. He suggested that SRA could either go and find another provider, or Alpha could build more capability. This gave SRA control of the decision and showed that Alpha's main priority was that SRA got the training they needed. He talked about the global contract and shared his surprise at the late addition of SRA. He acknowledged it was a tough job to pull off and explained the stress it had put on the Alpha team. He imagined it had been similarly stressful for SRA's team. He asked for time to try and get things right.

Over the next month they talked most days. It turned out that most of the issues could be sorted out by simply communicating more. Sandra was fearful that Alpha would take over complete control and that she would be sidelined. Infrequent communication had reinforced that anxiety. Training needs were identified, plans made jointly, and decisions over which trainers to use were discussed and agreed.

Joe paid another visit to Sydney. He met others within SRA. He went to dinner at Sandra's home. He told her about developments at SRA's regional HQ in Hong Kong.

And gradually, the relationship developed. In time, new faces were added to the Alpha team. Service improved. Joe became Sandra's eyes and ears at HQ. Within a year, Alpha were providing more than their fair share of training services to SRA and the Alpha and SRA teams worked together to get the best for SRA's employees – sometimes even collaborating to bypass the more impractical directives issued by Solve's US headquarters.

In the example above, the new executive on the SRA account was driven by a desire to help SRA – even if that meant admitting Alpha's failings. I Owe U sometimes demands this. The first step, whenever a relationship is not working, must be to understand the relationship you have currently. Once that has been done, consider what you can do to move the buyer. Below are some ideas for things you can try.

From social to partner

General

- Send the buyer relevant business commentary (e.g. newspaper articles) that you think might interest them. If it comes from your company, so much the better.
- Invite the buyer to social events with a technical element (e.g. product launches, conference cocktails, business chamber meetings).
- Get someone else from your organisation involved.
- Think about your contact network. Do you know anyone who the buyer might want to know?
- See if you can help them improve their relationships within their own organisation.
- Move meeting places to a more formal location.

Face-to-face

- Listen very carefully for any hints about areas where the buyer may not be 100% happy with their working life.
- Move the conversation to topics around how busy the buyer is, and to what it is that is making them busy. Ask questions about the things at work that they enjoy or do not enjoy.
- Ask about challenges at work. Ask what they have thought about doing to meet the challenges.

From ad-hoc to partner

General

- Ask if you can come and meet the buyer – not to sell but to get an understanding of what is going on in the business.

- During projects arrange meetings to discuss issues outside the project's scope.
- At the end of projects arrange a de-brief by the buyer on how the seller could have improved their level of service.

Face-to-face

- Focus on personal rapport.
- Be interested in the buyer's personal life – but only to the extent that they are willing to share, or to the extent that they show interest in yours.
- Ask about the business but also about their personal goals and challenges in the business.
- Talk about what you see happening in their industry and related ones.
- Focus on softly selling yourself (as someone who they would want to work with) rather than selling your company or offering.
- Ask permission to set this up as a regular event.

From technical to partner

General

- Call the buyer when you have nothing to sell.
- Invite them to social events (e.g. sports, theatre, opera).
- Hold some meetings in less formal settings (e.g. over lunch or coffee).
- Suggest a meeting to ensure your technical advice is dealing with the issue and not just the symptom.

Face-to-face

- Focus on ways to become less aloof and more accessible.
- Get to know the buyer personally. Ask about work pressure and work–life balance. Find out what they do outside work. Show interest.
- Tell stories of mistakes you have made, but not work related, to help break your status as an untouchable expert.
- Ask about the broader picture – the overall business strategy, market developments etc.
- Establish what sort of relationship this person has with their boss.

■ Resist the temptation to give technical advice – even when asked.
Respond with a question in order to get a better understanding.

The consistent theme here is that in order to change to a partner relationship you need to change your mindset to that of wanting to help.

Helping buyers' internal relationships

Within organisations we find that many relationships are ad-hoc or technical. This can be very frustrating for the more junior staff. This presents an opportunity for the I Owe U salesperson to help the buyer develop a partner relationship with their boss. If you can do this, the buyer really appreciates you helping them and they are then prepared to introduce you to their boss. This achieves two things for you. Your relationship with the first person deepens and you can start developing the relationship with the next person up the hierarchy.

A client of ours, Format Consulting, was trying to sell advice to Frederique Donat at Toxia. However, although Frederique knew that Toxia needed Format's help, she was concerned that her boss would think that she should be able to sort this out without seeking external help.

To get round the issue Format helped Frederique draft a letter back to Format saying that she was aware of new legislation and, whilst she had a broad understanding, she needed some detailed advice on the implications to Toxia. Frederique then got her boss to approve the letter and sent it to Format.

The result. Format got the work and Frederique's boss saw her as not only smart and up-to-date on legislation but aware of her own limitations. Everyone won.

3.4 A matrix of relationships

There are two sides of the coin with a partner relationship. From a personal perspective it is very good. If you change employer then the buyer will go with you. If the buyer changes employer then you will get the work from your buyer's new employer – in time. The problem is that you will not get the work from your buyer's old employer – unless you have fostered a similar relationship with other contacts at that company.

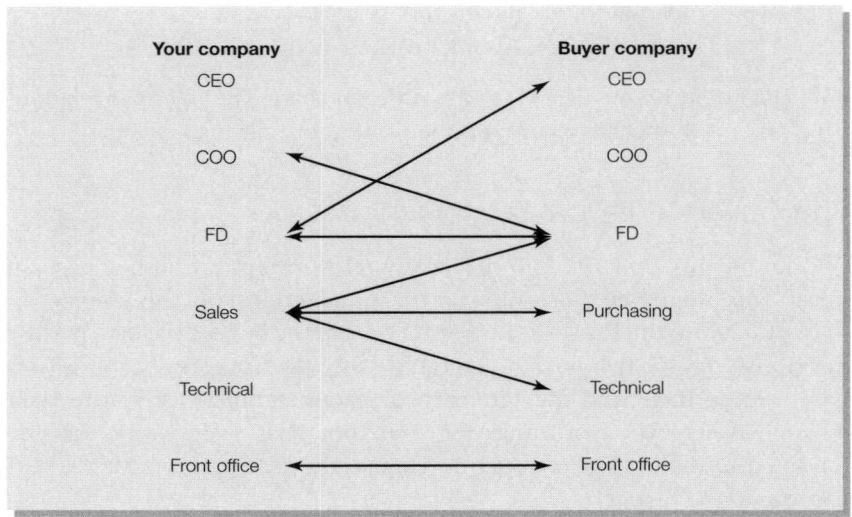

figure 3.3 **A relationship matrix**

The risk to your employer is that the buyer follows you and does not stay with your old employer. In which case the onus is on your old employer to ensure that more than one person has the partner relationship with the buyer. In an ideal world you should end up with a relationship matrix which looks something like the one shown in Figure 3.3.

This also provides for people moving up the hierarchy in each organisation so that as they become buyers the relationship is already in place.

You now have a better understanding of the types of relationship you can have with your buyers, and how to go about changing any relationships that you aren't happy with. We have, however, barely scratched the surface of how you need to behave in order to maximise the chance of success in shifting the relationship.

In the next chapter we look in detail at individual buyers – their types, roles and personal preferences – and how you need to adapt what you say and do, in order to establish rapport.

YarrA Limited – part 2

Richard and Emily spent the next few weeks analysing the conversations they'd had with Kiran and Rebecca over the years.

They realised that whilst Richard and Kiran had always got on well, the conversations had always been about fun things. They rarely got beyond the weather, the football scores, what the kids were doing and how busy they both were. With their new knowledge on classifying relationships, they decided the relationship with Kiran was a social relationship. It was fun, but not deep. It was enjoyable, but not important.

Richard concluded that he needed to elevate the relationship from *social* to *partner*. To do this he decided that the next meeting still needed to have a social element, but that it should be held in a more formal environment which would make talking about business much easier. He invited Kiran to have lunch at the local Thai restaurant and told him that he would really love to get a better understanding of Kiran's role at YarrA, and the company's business strategy.

Richard readily accepted. At the meeting there was the normal social opening but, very quickly, Richard changed the conversation from being about Kiran's social interests to being about what it was like for Kiran working at YarrA. Through the discussion Richard got a much better understanding of Kiran, how he operated and the challenges he faced. Kiran seemed to enjoy the opportunity to talk about work things to someone who seemed interested. At the end of the lunch Kiran said they should meet again in a month's time to talk again.

Emily, on the other hand, realised that she had only ever really been in touch with Rebecca when Rebecca called her, and when Rebecca had a problem that needed to be fixed. Emily had never really tried to understand the criteria that Rebecca was using to buy from her. Fortunately Emily had a great product at a great price so Rebecca had tended to buy from her. It was a reactive purchase and one based on quality of product or on price. On reflection, Emily thought this was somewhere between a *technical* and an *ad-hoc* relationship.

Emily called Rebecca and said that she realised that she did not really know enough about YarrA's business and that she would like to know more. Whilst initially taken aback by the call, because she did not need any help from Emily at that point, Rebecca agreed to meet Emily to get to know her better.

▶

They met in Rebecca's office. Emily opened the meeting by saying that it had occurred to her that the only time they ever met was when Rebecca had an urgent need, and Emily thought it may help her serve YarrA better in the future if she had a broader understanding of YarrA's business. That way, she might be able to put forward ideas before Rebecca had an urgent need, giving Rebecca more time to make sure she made the right decision.

Rebecca saw the value in this and for the next hour she talked about their growth plans and where she saw the greatest challenges. Emily learned a lot about Rebecca and about her business, and Rebecca appreciated being asked the questions when there was no purchase about to happen.

Emily and Richard met after their respective meetings with Kiran and Rebecca and compared notes. They concluded that whilst neither had yet developed a *partner* relationship, they now understood what they needed to do and they had started to move the relationship in the right direction in anticipation of the next need that Rebecca may have.

Key messages

- In order to change a relationship, you first need to understand what relationship you have at present.

- Seller–buyer relationships may be classified as ad-hoc, technical, social or partner.

- There are advantages and disadvantages associated with each type of relationship. I Owe U salespeople aim for *partner* relationships.

- Many salespeople overestimate the strength of their relationships with their buyers.

- Moving a relationship is often a matter of adopting a helping mindset and the right strategies – stopping to think before each interaction with the buyer and planning a consistent approach over time.

- Sometimes it is easier to introduce a new person in order to change a relationship than it is to break the current pattern.

4

Understanding and adapting to buyers

'Be not disturbed at being misunderstood; be disturbed rather at not being understanding.'

(Chinese proverb)

Organisational pressures to standardise approaches mean that buyers are sometimes treated as a homogenous group. Worse still, we have seen situations where marketing functions, far removed from the sales front-line, develop sophisticated (and costly) presentations that showcase the seller's offering and pass these to the sales team for implementation. The sales team are given little choice but to use these presentations in their sales calls despite knowing that such a 'one size fits all' approach is unlikely to succeed.

Others will pay more consideration to their buyers, but will make assumptions and act on those assumptions, often playing to business and cultural stereotypes.

I Owe U salespeople recognise that each individual buyer is different. They look for signals to understand individual buyers and then they test that understanding, remaining aware of their own behaviours and how those behaviours are likely to be perceived (see Chapter 2).

In this chapter we look at how to evaluate the different types, roles and personalities of buyers, so that as a salesperson, you invest both your time and energy in the brightest prospects.

Harbour Limited – part 1

Richard and Emily were hoping to win a significant new customer in Harbour Limited, a global organisation managing boat marinas. Harbour were looking for an all-in-one system that was integrated globally, thus allowing them to manage the whole business from their London HQ. They genuinely believed that the Apostle system could help Harbour achieve this goal.

Their meeting was with Mrs Choi and Mr Robbins – head of operations and head of IT respectively. Richard and Emily researched Harbour's industry and even established how long Mrs Choi and Mr Robbins had been in their roles. They also considered their own behaviours and were prepared to adapt them, should they need to.

They determined that they had no significant relationship with Mrs Choi since they had only met once. Richard though had some relationship with Mr Robbins, since they were both rugby fans and had been to a few games together. They were both determined to strengthen these relationships over the course of the next three meetings.

They met Mrs Choi and Mr Robbins at the coffee shop in Harbour's office building. Richard and Emily felt that the meeting went very well. Mr Robbins seemed very enthusiastic and did a lot of the talking, outlining Harbour's business strategy and the need for a consolidated back-office system. Mrs Choi did not say a lot, and seemed happy to sit and listen, letting Mr Robbins take the lead.

For their part, Richard and Emily listened carefully to Mr Robbins and then ran through a technical presentation prepared by FuturePerfect's Systems Team that illustrated how Apostle integrated with other IT systems. Emily was particularly pleased with the case study of a successful integration with Potential, the global HR system that she knew was used by all Harbour's offices.

A week passed after the meeting. And despite two messages Richard left for Mr Robbins they did not hear back.

Buyers come in many different shapes and sizes – how can a generic, standardised approach hope to be successful in addressing the complex needs of multiple buyers and organisations?

Of course, sometimes luck plays a part. The salesperson walks in to see the buyer at the precise moment when they need the seller's offering. It does happen – but not very often.

More often, the salesperson talks to a number of different people, presenting and re-presenting their ideas, but never reaching the point where a decision is made. This can be very time-consuming and very frustrating.

To save time, effort and blood pressure, it is helpful to consider four key questions when approaching buyers:

1   What is the organisation's approach to buying?

2   Within the organisation – what is each buyer's area of responsibility and degree of influence?

3   What is each buyer's role in the buying process?

4   What can we deduce about each key buyer's personality – and what can we do to make the process more comfortable for them (and us!)?

4.1 Different organisational approaches to buying

Just as individuals have different approaches to buying, so do organisations. Before deciding to invest the time and effort required building partnering relationships, it pays to make sure that the organisation values such a relationship.

I Owe U facilitates the building of profitable and sustainable relationships with buyers who attach value to being treated with trust, respect and care. Buyers who do not value these things will not respond to I Owe U.

Do such people exist? Definitely.

For convenience, we categorise buyers into one of three groups: price-busters, deal-hunters and value-buyers. Some of the features of each group are described below to help you identify them.

Price-busters	Deal-hunters	Value-buyers
■ No loyalty	■ Limited loyalty	■ Strong loyalty
■ Price is the only or major criterion	■ Price is a major criterion	■ Price is one of a number of important criteria
■ No face-to-face contact – all contact by phone and mail	■ Possible face-to-face, but not preferred	■ Face-to-face important as need to establish personal chemistry
■ Minimal attempt to understand provider's product, service, background or history	■ Some effort to understand provider's track record	■ Undertake detailed analysis of provider's capabilities and track record
■ Minimal information provided	■ Information provided – but on a need-to-know basis for the specific job	■ Lots of information – much of it strategic, sensitive and confidential
■ Standard contract terms	■ Standard contract terms	■ Flexible contract terms or no contract
■ Mistakes punished	■ Mistakes remembered	■ Mistakes forgiven

Types of organisation are as follows:

Price-busters	Deal-hunters	Value-buyers
■ Price-sensitive industries where margins are small (e.g. retail, transport, logistics)	■ Large, risk-averse organisations with strong internal control functions ■ Procurement functions ■ Government bodies ■ Public services and utilities	■ High-value brands ■ Professional services ■ Financial institutions ■ Financial services

Successful I Owe U salespeople tend to devote 80% or more of their sales time to value-buyers. Does this mean that you should ignore price-busters and deal-hunters? No, because the possibility of a change in leadership, strategy or ownership means that there is always the chance of their changing type. There may also be the opportunity to shift a price-buster or a deal-hunter to being a value-buyer. It is possible that they had not previously recognised or understood the full value of what they were trying to achieve. They may have been prejudiced by the way a previous seller interacted with them.

The key is to know how to spend the time that you invest. Our suggestions are that you focus on the following areas:

Price-busters	Deal-hunters	Value-buyers
■ Standardising your approach and minimising the cost of responding to requests and delivering your product or service	■ Taking advantage of any opportunity by exceeding the buyer's expectations and moving the relationship to one where they see your value to them	■ Since they know you, trust you and value the relationship, focus on expanding the relationship into new areas

Whilst writing this book Keith came across a very good example of the dangers of dealing with price-busters and a simple way you can change the buyer to a value buyer.

Keith recently bought a large plasma television. He researched the technical aspects and decided on the model he wanted. He then went to one branch of a large franchise home entertainment business. Let's call them Screens. They offered the television at $6,500.

He then went to four other Screens stores – all part of the same franchise network.

Each offered him the same product at a price to beat the previous best. He did buy from this company – for $5,700. The shop owner acknowledged he had only made $80 from the sale – he seemed happy however to have made the sale and 'beaten' the other Screens stores.

Some months later Keith decided to buy a new laptop computer. Again he did his research and identified a particular model he wanted. He went to three branches of Screens as well as four branches of another franchise organisation. Let's call them Boxes. The price in every branch of both stores was the same, give or take $20.

Keith then called the computer manufacturer's local office to see if they could beat the price. The employee he spoke to said they could not as it was a special deal they had with re-sellers. The employee went on to say that the price would be the same at all the re-sellers, but that he had heard that one particular organisation, let's call them MaxElec, was giving better after-sales support. Keith had never been to any branch of that firm in his life, but on the back of the recommendation he got in the car, went to the nearest outlet and bought the computer. And whilst he was there, he also bought a sandwich toaster.

In the first example above Screens made no attempt to move Keith from being a price-buster – in fact they almost encouraged it. In Octagon™ terms (see Chapter 2), the behaviour across the different shops was almost 'better than you' – in this case, 'better than other outlets in the same network'. In the second example, Screens and Boxes allowed Keith to remain in price-buster mode.

MaxElec, on the other hand, had clearly worked hard at building a reputation for service. With the help of the manufacturer's recommendation, they shifted Keith from price-buster to deal-hunter (since service as well as price was a key buying criterion).

Provided that the after-sales support lives up to Keith's expectations, there is the opportunity to build an ongoing relationship (loyalty) for all Keith's electronics purchases. This would be good for MaxElec, since Keith is about to buy a new house and he will need multiple air-conditioning units and all the electronics for a new kitchen.

Having worked out the organisation's approach to buying and the way to make best use of your limited time and resources, the next step is to think about the individual buyers within the organisation.

4.2 Buyer types and their influence

Miller and Heiman labelled three different buyer types in their book *Strategic Selling* back in 1987. The term 'economic buyer' is now part of the standard vocabulary of sales and is widely recognised as the person who 'signs the cheque' or, at least, is able to authorise the finance function to sign the cheque.

Two other buyer types were also introduced: 'user buyers' and 'technical buyers'.

The reason it is important to understand the different types of buyer is because each type can have an influence on the buying decision, and each is interested in different aspects of the sales proposition. To be confident of having 'covered all the bases' it is sensible to try to identify each type and their degree of influence in order to plan strategies to win them over.

The characteristics of the three different types are shown below:

Economic	Typical characteristics:
	■ Look for price performance, value for money, return on investment
	■ Responsible for bottom-line impact on the organisation
	■ Give final 'Yes' or 'No'
	■ Will work with the provider on a 'need to know' basis.
	Typical position:
	■ CEO/MD
	■ Finance Director
	■ Business Unit or Department Head.
	Risk areas:
	■ Product or service does not deliver the anticipated benefits
	■ Price paid for offering is seen as too high.
User	Typical characteristics:
	■ Look for impact on job performance and efficiency
	■ Will work with service providers on a day-to-day basis
	■ Personal success is linked to service, so they judge subjectively.
	Typical position:
	■ Business Unit or Department Head
	■ Line Manager.
	Risk areas:
	■ The offering does not deliver the anticipated operational improvements
	■ Implementation or use of the product is flawed leading to personal inconvenience and criticism from the organisation.
Technical	Typical characteristics:
	■ Look for measurable, quantifiable aspects of service offerings
	■ Like to appear objective and dispassionate
	■ Focus on the product or service itself – does it meet the detailed specifications?
	■ Screen out providers on the basis of technicalities; can give the final 'No'
	■ Make recommendations.
	Typical position:
	■ IT or other technical Director/Manager
	■ Procurement Manager.
	Risk areas:
	■ Offering does not interface smoothly with established systems and procedures
	■ Purchased product or service adversely affects existing systems or processes
	■ Competitors are perceived as having a better product.

Individual buyers often encompass more than one type – the most common being a single person who is both a user buyer and an economic buyer. In this situation, the buyer is interested not only in the financial implications of the offering, but also in the degree of inconvenience or benefit that use of the product or service involves, and the degree to which the success or failure of the purchase will affect their day-to-day work and career prospects.

The buyer type to watch out for is the technical buyer, whose influence is often underestimated or completely overlooked. Technical buyers such as IT functions, procurement departments and the like are often not directly involved in the interaction with vendors, and have no positive influence to bring to bear on the buying decision. What they can do is block a purchase. IT functions, for example, typically block the purchase of software that does not comply with the organisation's IT standards. A technical buyer can also be the economic buyer up to a certain cost.

It is a good idea, early on in the buying process, to ask the buyer who else is involved in the purchasing decision and to specifically reference any IT or procurement procedures. Of course, this should be done subtly – at a natural and appropriate time – preferably when you are already some way down the road to identifying that your offering is of benefit to the buyer. Ask too early and you risk undermining your buyer.

One word of warning. There is a danger that applying too much time and attention to analysing buyers can lead salespeople into the trap of viewing the buying process too much from their own perspective. For the I Owe U salesperson, understanding buyer types is a step on the path to understanding buyers' needs and motivations. Always remember that this analysis is a tool for increasing our understanding of the buyer's needs.

4.3 Roles

A further layer of complexity is added to understanding buyers by thinking about the different roles that buyers, and others that will be involved in the process, can adopt. The most common examples of 'buyer' roles during the sales process are as follows:

Sponsor	Typical characteristics:
	■ Supportive of you or your organisation's products or services in internal discussions.
	Who are they:
	■ Could be anyone at the buying organisation.
	Tactics:
	■ Give them the information they need to convince others
	■ Get them to help you meet others.
Anti-sponsor	Typical characteristics:
	■ Against you or your organisation's products or services.
	Who are they:
	■ Often the person within the buying organisation who should have thought of the idea
	■ Prior employees of your competitior
	■ Someone who is very cautious (see 4.4 below) towards change
	■ Someone who you have undermined in the past.
	Tactics:
	■ Provide information and examples to counter their spoken and unspoken concerns
	■ Beware!! – do not underestimate their influence
	■ Try to minimise their influence on the buying process
	■ Meet them and ask them what their buying criteria are.
Coach	Typical characteristics:
	■ Prepared to work within the buying organisation to help you win the job – often by providing information on key buying criteria and the perceived strengths and weaknesses of your offering and those of your competitors.
	Who are they:
	■ Your prior employees
	■ Staff seconded to work at the buyer's workplace
	■ Friends or relatives of staff working for the target customer.
	Tactics:
	■ Use them to gain intelligence on buying criteria, buyers' personal agendas, attitudes to you and your competitors.
Gatekeeper	Typical characteristics:
	■ Grant or deny access to the people and information you need.
	Who are they:
	■ Often secretaries and other administrative staff
	■ Technical buyers
	■ Procurement function
	■ Internal support functions (e.g. HR, IT, Marketing).

Tactics:

- They often feel mistreated or undervalued by their own organisation and outsiders. Be nice to them. Remember their names and chat with them when calling, before you ask to speak to their boss. Ignore them at your peril!
- Ask to see them personally
- Invite them to social events.

4.4 Personal preferences

Match for rapport and mis-match for action.

As we mentioned in the previous chapter, the I Owe U salesperson constantly strives to build a partner relationship. Once you have that relationship then your need to adapt the way you behave to a given individual is reduced. In the interim, however, it is your ability to adapt your behaviour that can be the single most important influence on whether you are able to build rapport and develop trust.

In Chapter 2 you looked at the way you behave (using the Octagon™ to assess your behaviour) and the way you come across to others. That is invaluable information but it is only half of the equation. Here we consider the buyer's behavioural preferences and the implications that has for how you might want to behave.

In many organisations you find that there is an ever-increasing percentage of staff who are a certain type. There is an obvious reason for this: people tend to recruit others like themselves. Why? Because they find these people easy to build rapport with.

The same logic applies to building rapport and trust in the area of sales. However, it is highly unlikely that you will have a salesforce that covers every personality type there is, and also have a system which makes it possible to allocate those with the right personalities to the appropriate targets. In which case, you are left with two options:

1 trust to luck or

2 learn to read other people's preferences and adapt your behaviour accordingly.

The latter approach can be hard work and, where your personality is very different from the buyer's, it may be preferable to get someone else involved. Unquestionably though, having the presence of mind to look for behavioural indicators in buyers, the means to interpret those indicators, and the ability to flex their own behaviours endows the I Owe U salesperson with greater resources in the quest to build rapport, win trust, and build deeper and more rewarding business relationships.

You cannot make changes to your deeper personality, but everyone has the capacity to adapt their surface behaviours. It could be argued that the buyer could also change their behaviour to adapt to your personality – but, of course, the emphasis is on you. You are the one trying to develop the relationship. Ultimately, the relationship may prove to be mutually beneficial – but as yet the buyer does not know that, so it is you who needs to adapt.

Reading and interpreting behavioural signals is an art, helped by a little science. Everyone is different, displaying a complex web of preferences, which are often in conflict.

The aim here is to develop sensitivity, since being more sensitive to the preferences of others can only improve our chances of establishing rapport.

Preferences	Signals	How you might adapt to build rapport with someone like this
■ Likes to think things through and prefers to analyse a problem fully before sharing the answer. ■ Is comfortable in their own surroundings and does not appear comfortable with other people.	■ Lots of silence in a meeting. ■ Takes time before answering questions, but when they do the answers have clearly been well thought through. ■ Declines invitations to business-related social events.	■ Force yourself to spend less than 50% of the time talking. Practise this with an observer. ■ Get used to leaving silence as it is, rather than filling it. ■ Try to ask very open questions. ■ Have one-to-one meetings, in a quiet place, at their office. ■ Be conscious that they may think the first thing that you say is a well thought out idea rather than something to discuss. Therefore, consider thinking through your ideas a bit more than you normally would, before speaking. ■ Talk slowly and gently. Do not invade their private space.

Preferences	Signals	How you might adapt to build rapport with someone like this
▪ Gets a thrill out of bouncing ideas with others. ▪ Thinks by talking and expects their ideas to be challenged and maybe changed. ▪ Gets their energy from other people. ▪ Likes meeting in public places.	▪ Lots of words, little silence. ▪ Seems to have endless energy. ▪ Many things they say are not necessarily correct.	▪ Try saying the first thought that comes to mind even though it may be wrong. ▪ Ask lots of questions if you are not comfortable with lots of statements. ▪ Suggest meeting in a coffee shop or other busy meeting place – they want to be part of the buzz! ▪ Engage them in debate, otherwise they may get bored.
▪ Likes to dream. ▪ Wants to start at the end and work backwards. ▪ Finds detail tedious.	▪ Uses graphics and pictures in reports or presentations. ▪ Rarely talks about facts. Mostly about impressions, concepts and vision. ▪ Makes big picture statements. ▪ Does not follow agendas.	▪ Keep the conversation flying at 40,000 feet. ▪ Use pictures to describe things. ▪ Use anecdotes and stories. ▪ Avoid asking for, or questioning, details. Ask questions more like 'And what impact will that have?' rather than 'Yes, but what about this element?'
▪ Prefers to refine the detail of what is already in place. ▪ Wants to plan from where we are now and take small steps ▪ Likes to be practical and realistic. ▪ Gets irritated by people with wild fantasies.	▪ Uses tables in presentations and reports. ▪ Always pointing out problems. ▪ Tends to talk sequentially – appears to think in steps.	▪ Ask questions to understand the person's immediate concerns, e.g. 'Currently, what are your three most important challenges?' ▪ Avoid statements such as 'This will save you millions'. You need to talk more about the current situation. ▪ Refer to vision and strategy.

Preferences	Signals	How you might adapt to build rapport with someone like this
■ Makes decisions based on what is fair. ■ Considers other people's feelings when making decisions. ■ Likes to discuss personal topics to better understand the other person.	■ Talks about personal issues. ■ Tends to use the word 'feel' rather than 'think'. ■ Talks about different people's perspectives. ■ Their decisions may not always seem logical.	■ You should be prepared to open up about yourself. They will want to know more about you, your life and your values, as opposed to the product or service you are selling. They will be happy to talk about personal issues – you need to match this. ■ Illustrate your thoughts by reference to their impact on people. ■ Focus on the benefits to the individual or group you are selling to.
■ Makes decisions based on what makes sense. ■ Focuses more on the facts and common sense than on the person. Likes to understand the situation rather than the person. ■ Focuses on the effectiveness and efficiency of the service or product.	■ Talks about 'facts' rather than 'feelings'. ■ Decisions appear to be based on logic. ■ Sometimes says things that appear insensitive.	■ Look purely at the economics and facts regarding the issue at hand. ■ Be careful about engaging in social or personal conversation. Discuss business issues to create common ground.
■ Likes to plan and organise. ■ Likes to know what is happening – does not like surprises.	■ Asks for agendas for meetings. ■ Sticks to the agenda. ■ Documents tend to show flowcharts or have lots of bullet points.	■ Send them agendas for meeting. ■ Talk them through when things will be done and be very logical. ■ Talk in very clear distinct patterns as if you are walking them through a flowchart.

Preferences	Signals	How you might adapt to build rapport with someone like this
■ Likes to free-wheel ■ Does not like planning for meetings, believing it makes it more natural to go with the flow. ■ The destination is important, the journey is not.	■ Conversations jump around from topic to topic. ■ Moves from one idea to another very quickly. ■ Documents and presentations do not have a logical flow.	■ Be prepared to move from one topic to another without resolution of the first. ■ Send objectives for a meeting rather than an agenda.

As we all know, no two people are alike, and the traits described above can often be apparent in the same person at different times, depending upon the situation, the dynamics of the group (e.g. in a larger meeting), or their mood on a particular day.

It can take years to master the skills of understanding and adapting, and even then you can be caught out. Humans can be so unpredictable! That said, an I Owe U salesperson equipped with an improved understanding of behaviours and able to read the signs is likely to be more successful than the person who goes from meeting to meeting presenting their ideas to very different audiences in a very standard way.

Although the techniques and awareness can take years to master, you can start the journey any time. One way to start is to take a second person to your meetings over the next few months. Their role is to listen and observe the buyer's behaviour – and yours. They should make notes on who said what, and note the reaction of the other person. They should also look for physical signals indicating personality preferences: tidiness; decorations; dress; photographs etc. Then, after each meeting, run through what happened and try to identify the buyer's type, role and preferences.

It is also important to recognise that people's behaviour can change, so there is a need constantly to check that any assumptions you have made, based on past assessments, remain valid. Specific events or changed situations (e.g. a new job, a promotion, changes outside work) can all affect a buyer's preferences and their reaction to your behaviours. For this reason, and because it sends good signals about the value you place on the relationship, we recommend periodic reviews of key buyers. A tool to help with this process is included in Appendix 5.

You should now have a better understanding of the type, role and preferences of the people with whom you are trying to develop relationships. In the next chapter we'll look at how an I Owe U practitioner builds rapport, the first step on the journey towards a trusted partner relationship.

Harbour Limited – part 2

Now that they understood the different types of buyers and the different roles they can play, Richard and Emily thought again about Mrs Choi and Mr Robbins.

They decided that Mr Robbins was the user buyer and possibly the technical buyer. Equally they realised that it was Mrs Choi who would approve the signing of the cheque. Since she was the economic buyer, they should have focused more on engaging her during the meeting. They also realised that they had focused on Mr Robbins because he was so open and enthusiastic – which made him a much easier person to deal with than Mrs Choi.

From his knowledge of Mr Robbins, Richard thought that they might have mis-read his role in the buying process. Initially Richard had thought he would be an active supporter but, on reflection, he realised that this was not Mr Robbins' style. He was more likely to help in the background as a coach, rather than be seen as an overt sponsor.

The key appeared to be to convince Mrs Choi that FuturePerfect were the right people to work with, to work with Mr Robbins to make sure that they stayed on the right track and to provide Mrs Choi with the comfort she needed.

They then thought about exactly how Mrs Choi behaved in the meeting and what she had said. She had not said much, and what she had said was in great detail. She also seemed concerned about what this product might mean in terms of new working practices and additional form filling.

A few days later, Mr Robbins called to say that they were not yet convinced that FuturePerfect's solution was the best fit for Harbour. Richard asked if they could meet again to discuss Harbour's concerns.

Richard suggested to Emily that this time she should go alone to the meeting. This would remove the impact of the natural rapport between Richard and Mr Robbins which may actually have

▶

marginalised Mrs Choi. Emily also asked if they could have the meeting in Mrs Choi's office (where Mrs Choi should feel more comfortable). Emily planned to talk about the specific details of the implementation path and the working practices that might be affected – highlighting the comprehensive training included and the initial dual operation of the legacy system and Apostle during the testing phase.

A remote observer of the meeting may have said that it was a bit dry and formal. Actually it was exactly what Mrs Choi wanted. She did not want to engage Emily on any level other than a professional one – and Emily matched her.

They talked briefly about the benefits of the software and spent more time discussing how the software might be implemented. Mrs Choi appeared particularly interested in the training element – and the step-by-step implementation path that Emily described.

That afternoon Richard received a call from Mr Robbins saying that Mrs Choi had been very impressed by Emily's attention to detail.

Key messages

- Every buyer is different. Do not rely on stereotypes.
- Understand buyer types – economic, user and technical – and the criteria they will use for buying and the influence they will have on the buying decision.
- Understand buyer roles – sponsor, anti-sponsor, coach and gatekeeper – and how best to manage them in your buying process.
- Think carefully about buyers' personalities and how you can adjust your behaviour to match theirs.
- Periodically ask buyers for feedback on their perception of the relationship with you and your organisation.

5

Building rapport and trust – the I Owe U approach

'You don't get a second chance to make a first impression.'

Anon.

An I Owe U salesperson signals their intention to help the buyer by establishing a collaborative environment as quickly as possible at the start of any conversation. In this chapter we look at how you do this.

Charterhouse Limited – part 1

As a result of feedback from a number of their buyers (see Appendix 3 for the feedback process), Richard and Emily now have a much better understanding of the way they are perceived by buyers. They also realise that for different types of people to 'want' to talk to them, they need to be able to flex their behaviour.

Always on the lookout for new opportunities, Emily noticed an article in the local newspaper indicating that Charterhouse Limited were looking to expand their operations. Emily had, as a result, called the CEO's secretary to see if they could arrange a meeting with the CEO, Bernard La Salle, to discuss if there was any way in which FuturePerfect could help Charterhouse with their expansion plans. After three phone calls and one 'accidental' meeting with the secretary in the sandwich shop close to Charterhouse's offices, Emily got an appointment.

On the way to the meeting, Richard outlined to Emily how he planned to open the meeting.

'Bernard is the CEO, so it is quite likely that he will be a "big picture" guy. I know he also does soccer coaching for kids in his spare time, so it may be that he is interested in helping others be the best they can be – or perhaps he just likes to help the kids win. We know he's a busy guy.'

'So,' Richard continued, 'I think we should have a four-point agenda:

1 Typical systems risks during business expansion
2 How Apostle software features help manage the risks
3 Implications of the software for people, processes and profits
4 Questions.

'This focuses on the things that Bernard might be interested in and puts priority on the impact the software will have on his people.'

Emily agreed that this seemed clear and logical. However, she did not feel entirely comfortable with the agenda. Worse, she could not explain why. She asked Richard to give her a few minutes to think about it and pulled over at the side of the road to go for a coffee.

5.1 Control and structure

Making the right impression the first time you speak to someone is critical. Get it right and the relationship has a greater chance of progressing smoothly. Get it wrong and you will either never have the relationship you want, or you will need to invest valuable time and energy trying to re-build a relationship that you could have started better.

David recalls a situation a few years ago when he and a colleague, Simon, were visited by two salesmen. They sat with these salespeople for an hour and had a very open and relaxed discussion about how their business was faring and the challenges they were facing. The salesmen made a reasonable attempt at asking the right questions and never once pushed their offering.

The following year they returned and there was a similar meeting. After the meeting, Simon asked David: 'What did they want?' 'No idea', David replied, 'It was a bizarre meeting.'

Next year, when the salesmen called to arrange the meeting, David and Simon made sure they were too busy.

It may well be that these people had an excellent offering which would have been of significant value, but they never stated their purpose and as a result David and Simon could not see any point in investing more time with them.

The key ingredients to creating the right first impression are:

▦ customer focus (as opposed to a focus on our own product or service)

▦ respect (for the buyer as a person)

▦ differentiation (what are you doing that differentiates your approach from your competitors).

In the previous chapter, we looked at the different types of buyer, their roles and their possible personality traits. We wrote about the need to understand their motivations. Now we need to be mindful of all these things, looking for clues that might aid our understanding, while we demonstrate to the buyer, early in our conversation, that we have respect for them and genuinely want to help them achieve their goals. We need to communicate that we are there to help with whatever challenges they are facing (business or non-business) – as opposed to the more common approach of being there to persuade, or even manipulate, them into buying our offering.

It is important to remember that many buyers have been hardened by the formulaic advances of other salespeople. They expect to be manipulated. Some even enjoy the game and set traps for unwary salesmen. Don't for example assume that everyone wants to start conversations by talking about their personal life and interests. Even if you and the buyer play golf, discussing their love of the sport in a business context may feel to them that you are encroaching on their personal space. Tread carefully.

Buyers have been conditioned by years of mistreatment to expect certain behaviour from salespeople and consultants:

'At best, they will tell me all about their offering and their company even though I have no interest in buying. At worst, they'll try to use some kind of scripted presentation to persuade or even manipulate me.'

I Owe U breaks this pattern, making even the most hardened buyer sit up and take notice. From the earlier chapters we've learned to understand our buyers and recognise that they have preferences and choices. One choice is whether they should see you or speak to you. By agreeing to do this, the buyer:

▦ gifts you their precious time – a part of their time on Earth that once committed is gone forever

▦ opens the way for you to ask questions that they may or may not want to answer

▦ acknowledges the possibility that they may need to give out information about their organisation or themselves – some of which may be sensitive

■ starts a process that may ultimately lead to them paying for your product or service.

As a result of this commitment from the buyer, the salesperson owes a debt and must give something in return. Hence I Owe U.

Here's what the I Owe U practitioner seeks to give in return:

■ control – letting the buyer drive the process, content and length of the discussion

■ structure – making efficient use of the time donated

■ insights and experience sharing – typically the most underused and undervalued asset in the salesperson's toolbox.

When we first introduce this approach, many salespeople say, 'We do this already.' So, we run a mock meeting and observe or record their openings.

Here is a typical example:

Social pleasantries. . . thank you for seeing me. . . followed by awkward silence when the buyer continues to give one-word answers, followed by a sudden switch by the salesperson to business issues.

'I know you're busy, so let me start by telling you something about our company. We are the [insert ranking] largest company in the industry and our business started in [insert year]. We employ [insert number] people in [insert number] towns/cities/states/countries and are recognised leaders in [insert field of expertise].

'Today I wanted to tell you about [insert product name or service].'

This opening achieves very little other than to confirm the buyer's suspicion that he is going to be sold to. Sometimes, of course, buyers have only themselves to blame. It is quite common to visit a buyer and have them say something like, 'OK, what have you come to tell me about today?' Faced with such a question, and the pressure of time, it is very tempting to get straight to the point and tell them about your offering. You have to be alert to miss the traps!

So how do you miss the traps? Principally by remembering that you cannot hope to successfully sell your offering if the buyer has not yet given any indication of their needs. The more complex and significant the product or service you are trying to sell (i.e. where there is some risk to the buyer), the more important this is.

In these situations, you have to first build an element of trust – or at least establish rapport – then find out how you will be able to help.

A good example of what *not* to do is often demonstrated by estate agents trying to get you to place your house for sale with them.

Keith recently sold a house.

Now, consider estate agents. It is hard to differentiate them. They all have windows that show the property. Their shops are next door to each other. They charge the same or very similar fees.

In such situations, the first meeting is absolutely crucial. It is the only time that the agent will be able to differentiate themselves. Keith will also allow them only five minutes, at best, to achieve that.

One agent last year started very well with Keith, and then blew it. He actually said at the start of the meeting, 'What do you want from your estate agent?' Keith was stunned. Maybe this would be different, maybe they would want to understand and help. Keith responded by saying, 'Feedback on comments from the public, advance warnings of house viewings and no pressure to drop the price every few weeks.'

The agent's response was, 'That is what everyone says,' and at that point he lost all credibility in Keith's eyes. Everyone does not want the same thing.

The agent then proceeded to spend 20 minutes going through a slide pack of exactly what they would do and how they were better than the rest. At no stage did he ask Keith what he wanted to get out of the meeting or even how long he had. The agent was oblivious to the fact that Keith's baby was screaming in the background and that Keith was up to his elbows in paint.

All he had to do was recognise and understand what was going on around Keith, and then ask what Keith wanted from an agent. From this meeting he could easily have won the job.

Moreover, since his offering turned out to be the same as everyone else's, he would actually have done better to keep Keith there for only 15 seconds and simply give him a bunch of forms to sign. That at least would have been a neutral experience for Keith, rather than a negative one.

5.2 I Owe U

The I Owe U approach advocated in this book derives from the mental tool that we use to set meetings with buyers on the path towards trusted long-term relationships. Here's how it works:

I is all about intent or aims. Explaining at the very start the reason why you are taking up your buyer's precious time. The key here is to try to express what you want to do in terms of how it will help your buyer. Better still, link your intent to some research that you have undertaken into the buyer's organisation or the industry. Which of the two openings below would you prefer to hear?

1 'We've just released a new network server that delivers a 20% improvement in network processing time and a 200% increase in storage capacity.'

2 'As you know, we build and sell servers. However I am not here to try to sell you one today. Instead, what I would like to do is find out what, if any, concerns you have with regard to data storage. One of my other clients recently told me that data storage and network congestion have become big issues as they move to digital document management. It occurred to me that document management might be a major challenge for your business too, so I thought that if I could get a better understanding of how you currently manage your paperwork, I might be able to offer some ideas on how you could do it better.'

Both approaches are fairly direct but the second approach puts the buyer at ease, knowing that they are not going to be sold to today.

Owe and specifically the 'we' reminds us that the meeting is a joint thing and that we will achieve a greater sense of collaboration if we try to hand over some control (generally the more the better) of the meeting to the buyer right at the start. Let's look at two options for setting out how to run the meeting:

1 'I prepared an agenda. First, let's discuss the volume of paper the company deals with, then how you currently manage that volume. Finally I can tell you something about our new network server. I've also left time for Q&As at the end.'

2 'First, thank you for taking the time to see me. How much time do we have?

'What I thought might be useful for both of us is first to talk about the key goals for the business and how this affects data storage. Then I can share with you some of the initiatives undertaken by other organisations that we've talked to and worked with.'

U is about focusing on the outcomes for the buyer and explicitly stating at the start of the meeting that you want them to get something out of the meeting. This is the part that communicates some *immediate* reward for them.

For many salespeople this is hard – usually because they undervalue their own experience. We're not suggesting here that something tangible can be offered – that is not usually possible. What is possible is to signal your intent that the buyer should get some intangible reward in the form of ideas, experience, contacts or some other useful information in return for the time they are committing and the confidential information they might discuss.

Again, two examples. One focused on selling and the other on helping the buyer achieve their goals:

1 'By the end of the meeting I should have a good understanding of the challenges you're facing and that will be the starting point for a long and mutually beneficial relationship.'

2 'During the meeting I will try to share some ideas and experiences from our work with other organisations. Hopefully that will be valuable to you, as it should help you either avoid the mistakes that others have made or, better still, lead you to think of better ways to attack the challenge. How does this sound to you?'

The distinction between the two examples is striking. In the first example, the seller stays in control. For many salespeople, this is a familiar and comfortable scenario. The second situation is not. What if the buyer says they want to talk about something that I don't know about, or an area where we don't have an offering that will help them? For the I Owe U practitioner this is a glorious opportunity. I can use my knowledge and my network to help my buyers in a way that they didn't think I could. They'll remember me!

Where people misunderstand U is that they make vague promises like, 'I hope we will be able to work together going forward.' This does not seek to reward the buyer for the *immediate* time they are devoting, so sounds to the buyer like a vague motherhood statement. It lacks impact and is open to misinterpretation.

Sometimes we get push-back around the intangible nature of the offer to provide insights. We're told it feels too weak, too uncertain.

Our response? Try it! It's different and it works. Too many sellers, starting from a point of intending to push their offering, feel uncomfortable about the way they sell. This leads them to underestimate the value of the insights and ideas that they have to offer. Organisations are always interested to hear about best practice and competitive intelligence. They will thank you for seeking to give it, and thank you even more if it actually occurs.

One of David's favourite relationship-building strategies is to refer clients to other consulting organisations that are expert in areas outside his areas of specialism. At the start of the first meeting with a new potential client he remembers to say something like:

'. . . and what I hope is that by listening to what you plan to focus on over the next 12 months, I can provide some insights into how I've seen other people approach similar issues and give you an idea of what works and what doesn't. I should also be able to recommend some names for you to contact if the topics are outside my specialist area.'

By the end of this type of meeting, where David has indeed shared ideas and contacts, he often hears the comment, 'You're different to other consultants.'

The reason I Owe U is so powerful as a way to open a meeting is because it is sufficiently different for the buyer to notice and it directs the meeting down a path of collaboration. It achieves very positive results for both buyer and seller:

Benefits for the potential buyer	Benefits for the potential seller
■ Sense of having control	■ Credibility aided by the buyer's
■ Understanding of what the	perception of your confidence at the
conversation is about	start of the meetings
■ Understanding of how the	■ Stops you talking too much and taking
conversation will run	control
■ Understanding of what they will	■ Involves the buyer and starts a
get out of the conversation	collaborative process

In today's business environment, if you can differentiate yourself from your competitors, simply by the way that you open a meeting, that is a big step in the right direction.

I Owe U is most effective in face-to-face situations, but the principle of giving away control is equally relevant to cold calling, as shown in the example below.

Keith frequently receives cold calls from two companies in Australia, where cold calling is quite common. Like most people his natural response is one of anger and frustration. However, the two companies have significantly different approaches and, as a result, attract two completely different reactions from Keith.

Company one is trying to sell Keith a time-share apartment. Their approach to the call is to start talking as soon as he picks up the phone and then talk, and talk and talk. Most often Keith just puts the phone down after about 15 seconds. Occasionally, however, Keith stays on the phone quietly getting angrier and angrier until they finish their script. At which point the salesperson at the other end asks for Keith's reaction and immediately regrets giving him the chance to say what he thinks! They have a 100% failure rate.

Company two is trying to sell Keith more or different telecommunications products and services. Their approach is to give Keith control very quickly. They give Keith permission to end the call within the first 10 seconds or so, and they do this in a very simple way. They ask, 'Do you have 5 minutes?' Most of the time Keith still says 'No'. About 30% of the time however Keith will say, 'No, but I do have 2 minutes.' Very occasionally he actually buys.

Whilst a 30% success rate may not seem significant, it is infinitely better than 0%. When Keith is given the permission to say that he does not have time, there is an almost physical reaction because he feels in control and that makes it more likely that he will agree to talk to them. If this can work for the seller in cold-call situations, then surely the passing of control in face-to-face situations must be well worth trying.

In the next chapter we look at how to move forward to help the buyer identify and prioritise any challenges they are facing – seeking to add disclosure, openness and sharing to the seeds of rapport and trust building planted through the use of I Owe U to open the discussion.

Charterhouse Limited – part 2

After a cup of coffee and a few minutes thought, Emily realised why she felt uncomfortable about the agenda Richard had prepared.

Although it was well-structured and precise, she could see a number of flaws:

- It put Richard and Emily in control of the meeting.
- It did not set out the time involved, or invite Bernard to discuss topics of interest to him.
- There was an implied assumption that Charterhouse is facing competitive pressures. This may have been true, but including it as an agenda item felt risky.
- They had assumed Bernard wanted to hear about their software.
- The whole agenda felt like it was centred around the software when the focus should have been on Charterhouse.

Emily talked to Richard and suggested they should try a different approach and not present a formal agenda. On arrival, Bernard's secretary showed Richard and Emily into his office and once they were comfortable, Emily started proceedings.

'Thank you for inviting us in and for setting aside the time. The reason we thought it would be useful to get together today is because we were reading in the trade press last week that Charterhouse is planning to expand production and open a new plant next year. We've worked with another client on their back-office systems for six new plants in the past few months and we thought it might be useful to see if any of the things we've learned would be useful to you.

'Your secretary told me on the way in that you have another meeting in 45 minutes, so I was thinking that the best way to use the time might be for you to start by telling us something about your expansion plans and any challenges you see in meeting the timetable you've set yourself.

'We can then talk about some of the projects we've worked on recently to see if any of the lessons we've learned apply to your situation. Does that sound OK, or were there any specific questions you wanted to ask us?'

Bernard replied that the outline sounded fine, so Emily finished off her introduction by saying:

'So, by the end of the meeting, we will have a good understanding of your plans and I hope you will have gained some insights from us, sharing our experience on similar projects, of the potential blocks and workarounds in relation to the IT systems at the new plant.'

'That would certainly be useful,' said Bernard 'shall I start?'

Key messages

■ Buyers expect that you will push them to buy.

■ Differentiate yourself from your competitors by displaying a strong desire to understand issues and share experience.

■ Use the I Owe U approach to start a collaborative journey by explicitly offering control of conversations to the buyer.

■ Reward buyers for the time they are investing.

6

Uncovering real needs

'He who asks a question is a fool for five minutes; he who does not ask a question remains a fool forever.'

Chinese proverb

A common analogy for the sales process is that it is like a dance. Buyer and seller circle each other (hopefully with some grace), before finally moving forward together – as partners. We have already discussed the tendency for the seller to take control – to take the lead and dictate the steps and the rhythm – and we have suggested that handing control to the buyer is a good idea.

Sellers often tango when a slow waltz would be more appropriate. Sellers assume they know what the buyer needs and they force the questioning process down certain avenues that they think will help *them* showcase *their* offering. The problem is that this is not a comfortable process for the buyer.

By contrast, I Owe U salespeople focus on helping the buyer; on delivering value to the buyer from every interaction. One way they achieve this is through the use of a powerful enquiry process that helps buyers clarify their priorities. This chapter introduces the SHAPE enquiry process and the Value-Sheet, core elements in the I Owe U practitioner's toolkit.

Integrated Architects Ltd – part 1

Chris Schumacher, the Operations Partner of Integrated Architects Ltd, called Richard and Emily to say he had seen FuturePerfect's advert about the new Pilot system and he wanted to know more,

▶

since Integrated Architects were considering replacing their current purchase control system.

Richard and Emily learned everything they needed to know about Chris. The role he had, the type of person he was, his buying criteria.

The meeting was held in Chris's office and took well over the hour for which they had planned. Richard explained the detailed specifications of the new Pilot system to Chris, and discussed the cost and implementation options. Chris asked questions about the system and about FuturePerfect's track record, so he was clearly interested. Emily told Chris the names of all the companies they had worked with in the past, which was an impressive list.

Richard thought they were very thorough and that the meeting went really well. Emily was not so sure. She thought they might have spent too much time talking about Pilot and not much time understanding how Integrated Architects would actually use the system. The air-time split was around 70% them, 30% Chris.

She thought Chris was happy with what they had to say about the product, but she was concerned that he gave no signals that he was ready to buy.

6.1 Personal power

A useful starting point for understanding the dynamics of seller–buyer interactions is an understanding of something we refer to as personal power. On the positive side, people take comfort and draw strength from

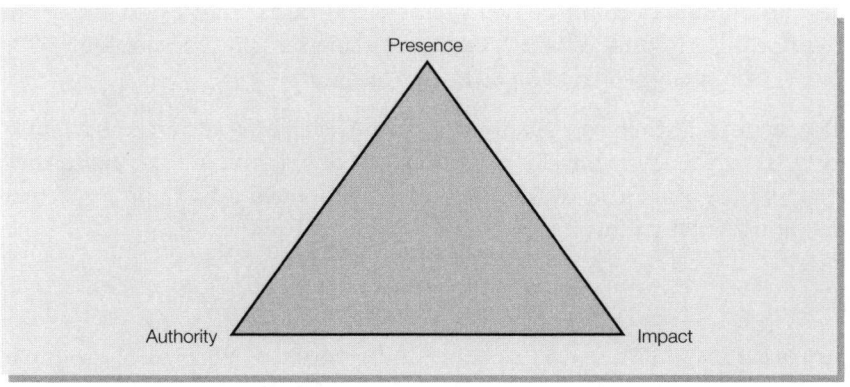

figure 6.1 **Personal power**

their personal power. Unfortunately it can also play a big part in blocking a person's ability to understand others.

Personal power derives from a combination of three factors, as shown in Figure 6.1.

Presence

Presence is almost physical. You can improve your presence but to a large extent, you are born with it. People with 'presence' get their comfort from attraction.

Many influential people, including a number of politicians, possess significant 'presence'. Former US President Bill Clinton has built a remarkable career leveraging his 'presence'.

However, from a relationship perspective, it can be hard to develop partner relationships with 'presence' only. Whilst 'presence' tends to attract others, it can also be intimidating. Further, whilst 'presence' can impress at the start of a relationship, a buyer may start to feel, over time, that they are not getting sufficient value from the seller. A typical reaction might be:

'While they may look good, they do not change my thinking (impact) and they don't appear to know as much as I first thought (authority).'

Authority

Authority is knowledge. It is about the brain. It links to what you know, who you know, where you have been. People with 'authority' take comfort from 'knowing'.

People working in technical fields tend to get their comfort primarily from 'authority'. IT professionals, engineers, lawyers and accountants, for example, usually sell from a position of 'authority'.

If you put together two people who base their personal power on 'authority' they will try to out-do each other. Not only is one of them right, they are 'righter' than the other. It is almost impossible to build a partner relationship when this happens.

Impact

Impact is the ability to create change in the moment through engagement and questioning: the catalyst. People with 'impact' take comfort from engaging others.

Many influential people within government and business leverage their impact skills. It is the skill itself which makes them influential. They use their skills to challenge the current vision, strategy and plans through asking incisive questions.

Why develop impact skills?

Developing a solid understanding of your buyer's needs is critical to successful selling. Our experience shows that many salespeople fall into the trap of talking about their product or service before they fully understand a buyer's needs. This demonstrates a self-bias as opposed to a buyer focus and can lead to disastrous results.

What buyers repeatedly tell us they want is someone who can help them in every interaction. Someone who, at some stage in every interaction, creates an 'aha' moment. This is someone who operates using impact skills.

For the rest of this chapter we look at a range of tools and processes to help increase the level of comfort you get from your ability to create impact. This will not only increase your ability to understand buyers' needs and build partner relationships, it will also improve your confidence and performance in those critical situations where you do not possess the answer.

6.2 Introducing SHAPE

Figure 6.2 shows our SHAPE model. The SHAPE enquiry process (Figure 6.2) seeks to align the seller's questions with the direction of the buyer's thoughts (see Figure 1.2).

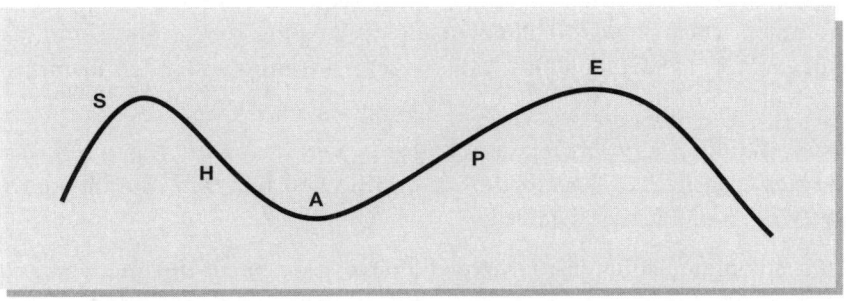

figure 6.2   **SHAPE model**

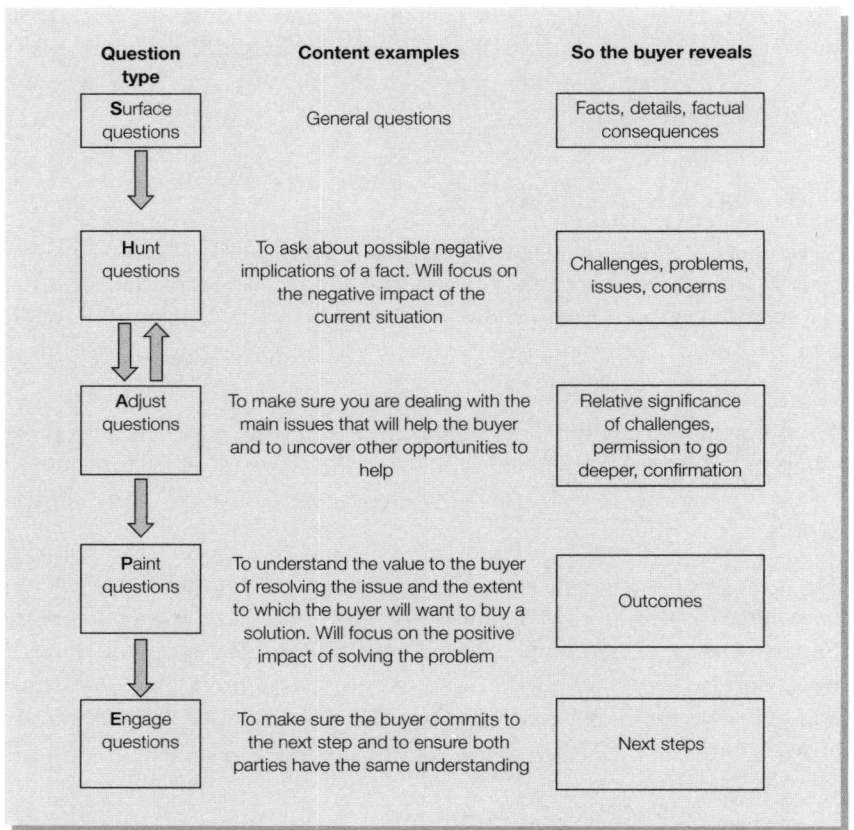

figure 6.3 **SHAPE process**

In overview, the SHAPE process is as in Figure 6.3. While the arrows in Figure 6.3 indicate the typical sequence, this is not set in stone. Indeed, in the course of any interaction, the entire sequence, or parts of it, will be repeated when discussing different topics. Looping back is also common, for example to **Surface** additional facts once a **Hunt** question has identified a challenge or problem.

You should not, however, use **Engage** questions until the buyer has expressed a need. Allied to this, it is critical to recognise the difference between a problem and a need.

It is a common reaction to interpret a buyer's statement of a problem as a statement of need. Deeper consideration reveals the difference between a problem and a need. On any day, each of us faces a number of problems or challenges – both in our personal and professional lives. Some things we decide to change that day, others we allow to linger. Some turn out to be not a problem at all, or just the symptom of a bigger problem. So it is with buyers. Problems do not equal needs. A need is where the buyer tells you that they not only have an issue but that they want it resolved.

With this basic understanding in place, we will now explore each stage of the SHAPE process in more detail.

6.3 Surface (the facts)

'There is a big difference between listening and waiting your turn to speak.' (Anon.)

Surface questions ━━━━━▶ *Facts*

Too many meetings between sellers and buyers begin with an assumption on the part of the seller that there is a problem that they are there to solve. A consequence of this assumption is that meetings move too quickly into potentially negative areas, i.e. talking about problems. The seller then falls into the trap of promoting their offering too early.

A spectacular failure

A firm of business consultants was requested to bid for a piece of work with a large Chinese enterprise. In order to show their serious intent, the advisors decided to fly five of their most senior employees to Beijing to meet the client and demonstrate their capabilities. The meeting, held in the company's boardroom, began with formal introductions and then moved into a presentation.

After 15 minutes it was interrupted. The Chairman of the meeting requested the consultants to pause their presentation and speak with him outside the room. He told them that they had clearly not understood what was required and that the presentation was not addressing their needs. He suggested they returned home, take another look at the information that they had been given, then return and present again.

Double jeopardy! Not only had they created a poor impression in the prospective client's mind – having demonstrated a failure to understand the buyer's needs – they also had to incur the costs of returning to present again and the time involved in rethinking their approach.

The consultants were not happy, but they had only themselves to blame. They had fallen into the trap of assuming they knew the answer – and they presented their answer – without fully understanding the buyer's needs.

How would an I Owe U salesperson have approached this? First, they would have used I Owe U to start the meeting. At that point the buyer would have advised them that this was not the process he wanted for the meeting. Second, after the I Owe U they would have checked their understanding of what was expected by asking a few well chosen **Surface** questions.

So, the next step after an I Owe U introduction is to move into **Surface** questioning. These are neutral questions that seek to acquire knowledge. They do not infer or suggest there are any problems. This is important. One of the biggest obstacles a lot of salespeople appear to face is simply having conversations with potential buyers where there may be no 'problem' being discussed. This goes back to the very heart of being an I Owe U salesperson. The seller should be talking to the buyer even if they may have no immediate problem to resolve.

Surface questions are designed to prise information, ideas and thoughts from the buyer. It is as if there is a rock stuck in the soil and you are trying to get it out. What you are trying to do is not smash the rock, but loosen the soil around the edges.

Surface questions get the buyer to talk about facts. Examples are provided below, together with the responses they typically elicit:

Surface question	Response
How is business going?	You know how it is, ups and downs. **Fact**
How busy are you this time of year?	Extremely busy, it is our peak period. **Fact**
What are your three key objectives for the next year?	Profit, more profit and yet more profit. **Fact**
How do you think you are faring compared to the competition?	I think we are OK. I suspect we are all in the same boat. **Fact**
What is customer feedback like?	Generally it is fine. One never gets perfect feedback. **Fact**

Follow-on **Surface** questions are along these lines:

- 'How do you currently track sales?'
- 'Can you tell me more about that?'
- 'Can you give me a bit more idea exactly how that works?'

As the conversation progresses the buyer may hint that there are some areas where everything is not 100% perfect. This is a danger point. There is a temptation to dive straight in at the first sign of a potential issue. Much better is to think back to exactly what the buyer said about the topic – where there may be an issue – then consider asking one of two types of question to test the degree of need.

If you look for more facts and explanation, then you are asking another **Surface** question. For example:

'A few minutes ago you mentioned that profit margins were not as high as you had expected. Do you have any idea what is causing this?'

You are likely to get more facts in response.

Alternatively you could decide to ask a **Hunt** question such as:

'A few minutes ago you mentioned that profit margins were not as high as you had expected. Is this a concern?'

This question does have a negative connotation. It pushes the buyer to talk about a problem or challenge – and that is what makes it a **Hunt** question.

6.4 Hunt (for challenges)

Before we get into the detail of **Hunt** questions we should remind ourselves that we are looking to help the buyer identify and resolve any challenges that are of significant concern to them. Not those challenges that are of significant concern to you.

You might think that the buyer knows what their challenges are. That is not necessarily the case. Buyers sometimes know that they have a problem, but are so preoccupied dealing with the latest deadline that they never get around to thinking seriously about long-standing issues and problems.

The framing of issues and the ability to put issues into context is something that a person who is close to an issue cannot always do. Think about your personal experiences – often when you cannot work something out, simply talking about your issue with someone else makes things seem better. It is the same in business, and many salespeople underestimate how much buyers can benefit, simply from talking through an issue and hearing a different perspective.

You may now be thinking, 'OK, so I've helped them understand the issue. If it is not in my area of expertise or if it is not something that my product can solve then how can I help?' It is possible that you cannot help. It may be that you do not even have any ideas about who else could help – but there is a good chance that you will be able at least to provide some direction. Let us give you an example:

Two for one

A client of Keith's, Taxad, was trying to sell some tax advice to one of their clients, Bluem, but they could not understand why Bluem was not buying. It was clear that the work needed to be done and Taxad was the obvious choice to do the work.

They called Keith in to try to unearth what was happening. It was not that hard to find out. Keith asked Bluem, 'What is the biggest challenge you face at present?' To which Bluem responded, 'We have just moved to the suburbs and are having real problems communicating effectively with our suppliers and our customers.'

Taxad then offered to get their technology people (not something they sold) to talk to Bluem about what options they may have. Simple enough – and it worked. Bluem got their challenge resolved, Taxad was seen to have helped them resolve it, and the tax work was given to Taxad.

Some examples of **Hunt** questions and possible responses are:

Hunt question	Response
Does that have a negative impact on your bottom line?	Yes, <u>unfortunately</u> it is reducing our net profit by 10%. **Problem/Challenge**
How unhappy are you with the import duties that you pay on that?	Very, it is <u>messing around</u> with our cashflow. **Problem/Challenge**
And does the down time for the machinery cause any problems?	Yes, it means we have people we are paying for <u>doing nothing.</u> **Problem/Challenge**
Does using more than one supplier lead to any communication issues?	Yes, we are <u>forever behind deadlines</u> because the suppliers don't talk to each other. **Problem/Challenge**
And is the short life span of the material a concern?	It is, because we are always having to re-fit – and that <u>costs</u> money. **Problem/Challenge**

The difference lies in what the buyer says. In all the above responses, they have expressed that they are worried or have a concern (see underline). **Hunt** questions seek to understand whether something that is happening is perceived as a problem or concern.

One you have identified an issue or concern you need to understand its significance. You also need to help the buyer understand, so that they decide whether or not this is a sufficiently big challenge that it needs to be addressed.

Help the buyer think about the scale of the challenge, what knock-on impact it could have and any other negative consequences that may or may not have been considered previously. For example:

Hunt question	Response
Are there any other knock-on effects this has?	Yes it is starting to lead to some negative customer feedback. **Bigger challenge**
Does this reduced profit have any impact on your ability to spend on R&D?	I had not really thought about that – yes it does. **Bigger challenge**
What impact does this have on staff morale?	I guess it does not help. Now you mention it our staff turnover has increased. **Bigger challenge**
What other impact does the down time have on the business other than the staff cost issue?	It can cause problems with meeting deadlines. **Bigger challenge**
And what are the three biggest impacts on the business of the unreliable equipment.	My stress level, irritated staff and cashflow. **Bigger challenge**

We have been involved in many projects where the seller says that they *know* that they have the answer to their buyer's issue, but still the buyer will not buy. Often the reason is that while the issue you are trying to solve could be important to the buyer, it may not be the *most* important challenge they face.

Sometimes you ask a **Hunt** question in order to identify a problem, but the buyer simply acknowledges what you see as a problem to be merely a fact. At this point, ask **Surface** and **Hunt** questions to either:

■ identify whether there are more negative consequences to the fact than the buyer may have at first realised – and thus it becomes a challenge, or

■ see whether there are any other issues or problems.

More to this than meets the eye

A very experienced legal advisor was once confronted with a situation that he could not understand. He advised a property development company that it could undertake legitimate planning that would save it millions of dollars in tax charges. The steps needed to secure the tax advantage were relatively straightforward.

To the advisor's amazement, his client decided not to pursue the opportunity. The advisor could not understand it and ultimately branded the client as 'stupid'.

In fact, this was not the case at all. The advisor's client was simply considering other variables. They viewed the paying of taxes as a 'fact of life' and they were quite comfortable with the level of tax they paid. For them it was not a problem. Moreover, a necessity for operating a successful property development business was the maintaining of good relationships with government officers. The developer did not want to risk their good standing with government by taking a quick reduction in their tax burden.

Remember too that even if you cannot solve the biggest issues the buyer faces, it is in your interest and your buyer's interest that you help them understand and resolve those issues. There are two reasons why this approach is key:

■ Once the buyer has resolved the issue that you cannot help with directly, they can move to the issue that you can help with.

■ The buyer will appreciate that you have been helping them, even when there is nothing in it for you, and they will trust you and want to work with you again.

So to summarise, **Hunt** questions uncover the buyer's biggest issues and help you and the buyer understand how big each issue really is. This leads on to identifying the most important challenges from among the many issues and problems (see Sections 6.10 and 6.11).

6.5 Adjust (to signal direction)

Adjust questions  *Prioritisation*
Permission

This is the most counter-intuitive step in the SHAPE process – but potentially very helpful to the seller and the buyer.

Now, although **Hunt** questions solicit a negative response about the current situation, the buyer has not yet said that they want to resolve the issues under discussion, regardless of how big they appear. The seller cannot be sure yet that they are dealing with the buyer's biggest challenge.

Once you have found an issue which is clearly of concern to the buyer, it could be very tempting to keep digging, and then push the buyer to solve it. There are two possible risks at this stage.

1   It may well be that whilst the issue is of concern to the buyer they may have even more pressing issues. You need to deal with those. Sellers need to be particularly careful where the first issue that was discussed happens to be the one for which the seller can provide a solution. This should raise a question in the seller's mind as to whether they subconsciously directed the conversation in that direction. Equally, has the buyer moved in this direction because they see the seller as one-dimensional and only able to push their own solution? Before proceeding, the seller needs to make sure that this is the key issue for the buyer.

2   If this is a key issue to the buyer then you may be treading on thin ice. This could be an issue about which the buyer is sensitive and you need to confirm they are happy for you to proceed down this line of questioning. The chances are that they will be OK with this, but it shows respect if you just check first.

Only the salesman was excited

We recently heard of a house builder, James, who had been talking to the Williams family for several weeks about the possibility of building their house. He had a great reputation in the local community for building very solid houses that appreciated in value.

Over the weeks James had asked all the right questions to identify that the Williams family were looking for a well-built house which would also prove to be a good investment.

They had a meeting arranged for a particular Saturday on the plot of land where the house was to be built. To James's amazement, about half an hour before the meeting he received a text message on his mobile saying they could not meet him. There was no reason and no re-schedule details. James tried to call them immediately, but their phone appeared to be switched off.

A few days later, James received a second text message which explained the first message. The Williams family had decided to use another builder. It was a builder that James knew very well. Relatively new to the market, but who was selling the fact that he specialised in eco-friendly houses. James rang the other builder who said that Mrs Williams was a peace activist and member of the Green party and her prime objective for the house was that it should be eco-friendly.

James could build very eco-friendly houses, but he had never slowed down the questioning process to ask whether having a solid house which would appreciate were the key issues that the Williams family had in mind when it came to building their house.

If he had just asked one **Adjust** question, rather than get excited that another possible buyer wanted what he specialised in, he would almost certainly have won the contract.

Adjust questions direct the seller to check that they have identified a key issue or challenge. They also give the seller and the buyer time for a breather. They change the pace of the conversation and everyone can relax for a few seconds.

Here are some examples:

Adjust question	Response
In terms of your overall objectives how important is this issue?	This is the key concern at present. **Confirmed key issue**
Is this the most important concern facing you at present?	It is a big issue but to be honest there is one other which is causing me sleepless nights. **There is a bigger issue**
Would your CEO agree that this is the key challenge at present?	Absolutely – he mentions it several times a day. **Confirmed key challenge**
This issue seems close to your heart, are you happy for us to continue discussing it?	You are right, it is close – but yes, please continue. **Permission**
I can see that this is a sensitive area, are you happy to keep talking about it?	Assuming confidentiality then yes, I am happy to talk about it. **Permission**

Adjust questions solicit from the buyer the relative importance of an issue or permission to continue a line of questioning. If the buyer says there is a bigger issue, then you need to resort to **Surface** or **Hunt** questions on that issue. If the buyer confirms that this is the key issue or gives you permission then you still have two options:

1   You can suggest that you will come back to this issue later, and start asking **Surface** questions for more context or to dig around for other issues.

2   You can ask more **Hunt** questions on this issue before moving to **Paint** questions.

If you decide to pursue this issue, remember you are still not in a position to sell. The buyer has not said they want to resolve the issue. This comes through the **Paint** questions covered below.

6.6 Paint (for positive future outcomes)

Paint questions ➡ *Outcomes*

Paint questions are a key differentiator of the SHAPE process. Most salespeople are trained in and skilled at identifying issues. Many can move from issues to needs. Few are skilled at building a positive picture of life after the issue is resolved. The **Paint** step is missed too frequently by salespeople and it is an important step, since people feel much happier buying into a bright future than a negative present!

Once you have confirmation that you are talking about the key issue, you are confident that all the negative implications of the issue have been raised and understood, and you have permission to keep talking, then it is time to change direction – or at least language and emphasis.

At this stage the buyer owns the problem but may or may not own the need to solve it. For example, they may see a problem but feel that the solution is beyond their control. You need to make sure that full ownership rests with the buyer.

To do this you move from building the negative aspects to helping the buyer **Paint** a brighter future. Painting the future focuses on the positive outcomes of addressing the issue or problem and helps transform it to a challenge that demands action.

A painfully long process

Elaine is one of the most experienced salespeople for All In One, one of the largest manufacturers of software systems for large organisations. Their software handles all aspects of a business: finance, human resources, time management etc. For four months she had been in negotiations with Marcus, the Chief Operating Officer of Plaisir, a French-based manufacturer of all types of home electronics.

Elaine was fairly convinced that she had won the work. Marcus had even told her many times that they were not considering using anyone else. She and Marcus had talked at length about all the problems Marcus had with Plaisir's current status. Lots of different systems, duplication of inputting data and unreliable software. Marcus acknowledged how much it was costing them and how incredibly frustrating it was.

Four months after Elaine had put forward a proposal, including costs, there had been three further meetings to discuss the proposal and implementation – and still they did not appear to be any closer to getting a signature than they had been four months earlier.

At each meeting they revisited old ground. They talked about all the problems that were getting bigger by the day – and still no signature. The only thing that had changed was that Elaine had dropped the price by 5% to try and close the deal.

Rebecca, Elaine's boss, was tired of hearing her say that next month it will be a done deal, so she stepped in. Rebecca attended a meeting that Elaine had arranged with Marcus. The meeting lasted about 45 minutes and at the end of the meeting Marcus asked Elaine when they could start the implementation. The contract was signed within a week.

At the first planning meeting with Marcus, Elaine asked why he suddenly decided to start. He said that up until that meeting all he had really focused on was how big his problems were – and by the end of each meeting he generally felt very depressed and overwhelmed. At the meeting with Rebecca suddenly all he was seeing was how good life would be when the new system was implemented.

Here are some examples:

Paint question	Response
What would be the impact of resolving this?	It would reduce our down time in the office and improve morale. **Outcome**
To what extent would resolving this help you?	It could grow the bottom line by as much as 15%. **Outcome**
What would be the cash value of solving this?	Significant, upwards of $500,000 per annum. **Outcome**
What would be your ideal situation regarding this?	I would like the communication to happen without my constant involvement. **Outcome**
What would you like to achieve?	I would like to reduce the turnaround time to one week. **Outcome**

With **Hunt** questions you work to understand all the negative implications of a challenge. **Paint** questions help the buyer to understand all the positive implications of resolving a challenge and to appreciate the total value – tangible and intangible – of action. They have to really want to take action.

Paint question	Response
I just want to remember what all the upsides of this would be.	It would reduce our down time in the office and improve morale. **Big outcome**
So as well as affecting cashflow, this will reduce the negative feedback from buyers – is that right?	Yes it would and that would be great. **Big outcome**
Can I just confirm that if you manage to deal with this it will not only help motivation, it will also improve profits and reduce your stress levels?	Yes that is right, we really do need to resolve this now. **Big outcome**
So you would like to solve not just the turnaround, but reduce the cost base as well?	Yes, if we could achieve that my life would be a lot easier. **Big outcome**
And if we could get the turnaround down to a week what would that mean to you.	It would increase profit and morale and would please the CEO. **Big outcome**

You will note that there are two different styles of **Paint** questions above. One which is more of an open question and one which is more directive. We prefer the open question, but sometimes you need to be more directive. The key is that by the end of the process the buyer 'owns' the outcome. You can judge this as much by a buyer's emotional commitment as by the words they use.

Once the buyer has stated the outcome they want, you have moved the relationship to the extent that they will use you when they can. The conversation itself has been a very positive experience for the buyer and they trust you more than they did at the start. You have not tried to sell them anything, but you have helped them move their thinking and move towards resolving one or more of their key challenges.

The next step is where you get commitment to action. This may be action you will take or action the buyer will take.

6.7 Engage (to move to action)

Engage questions ━━━━━━━━━▶ *Next steps*

Once the buyer has decided to do something, and hopefully urgently, the next step may just happen, but you need to make sure it does happen.

There are two key dangers at this point:

1 An assumption is made that the deal is done and plans are made to deliver the offering, when in fact the buyer does not feel that they have made a firm commitment.

2 The seller moves to 'close' the deal.

Wasted investment

Pieter was extremely surprised at how quickly Tula had decided to buy his web site development package. They had only had two meetings and Tula had already asked for a proposal. They had agreed a price and also all the specifics of the web site. This was a huge project for Pieter.

Pieter assumed that the reason the process had been so fast was that Tula had come to him and knew she wanted a web site – and she wanted it quickly. Pieter had a decent reputation and also understood what Tula was trying to achieve.

The only problem Pieter had was that he knew he did not have all the right resources to build the web site, and when the contract was signed he would have to get the site up and running very quickly.

Pieter decided the only option was to recruit two new web developers and buy some new equipment. This he did, and within a couple of weeks his team had doubled and he had bought the new equipment.

The next time Pieter met Tula he walked in very excited and left devastated. He told Tula about the investments and Tula responded by asking why he had assumed that the contract would be signed. At no stage had Tula said she would definitely buy. Pieter had not even asked the question.

Regardless of how well the sales process goes, asking **Engage** questions increases the level of certainty that the sale will go through.

Here are some sample **Engage** questions:

Engage question	Response
Would you like us to help you resolve this?	That would be very helpful. **Next step**
Would you like us to put forward an action plan for helping you?	When would you be able to do that by? **Next step**
Would you like me to start work on this now?	Next week would be fine. **Next step**
Do you know who might be able to help you resolve this?	I think that our internal team will need your help. **Next step**
Would you like me to see if I can find someone who may be able to help you?	If you would be able to find someone that would be great. **Next step**

This is not the end of the process – for the I Owe U salesperson it is reaching first base. It is vital that you follow through on any promises, confirm what you have discussed and agreed, and maintain the interest of the buyer. We cover how to do this in later chapters.

6.8 Summary of SHAPE and tools to assist your learning

Mastery of SHAPE questioning is the key difference between a good salesperson and a truly great relationship builder. It is the skill that maximises the value that you give to your buyer in every interaction between the two of you.

Reading this book is the start of a learning process. To master the skills, such that asking the right type of question at the right point in the meeting becomes second nature, takes time and practice.

We recommend a three-stage process towards mastery:

1 Observe and listen to others. Learn to identify the different types of question in the SHAPE process. Note down the good examples that you hear. Write your own examples.
   To set you on your way you will find some tests and answers in Appendix 5. You can try these now to see if you already have a good understanding of the process.

2 Practise the skills in safe environments – on family, friends or work colleagues. Observe the responses you get and ask for feedback, focusing on whether your questioning appeared natural, comfortable (for them) and focused on their needs.

3 Finally, try them with buyers. Start with a buyer with whom you have a good relationship or with one whom you have no relationship. Take a colleague to meetings and get feedback from them afterwards on which questions you asked and what the buyer's response was. If you have a friendly buyer, you might even ask them about their reaction to the meeting process – being careful to phrase your questions to show that you are using the process to assess whether this is the best way to run the meeting so that they get the help that they need.

There are additional free resources to aid your learning available at www.ioweu.com.

6.9 An easier SHAPE

When we work with groups of salespeople and introduce them to SHAPE, we often get pushback:

■ 'It takes too long.'

■ 'Our buyers don't want to talk about this stuff.'

■ 'Our buyers don't have the authority to talk about big issues.'

■ 'They just want to know the price.'

Faced with these reactions, we first acknowledge that not all buyers will have the time and interest to have deep conversations with salespeople. Then we ask whether they have tried? The answer is almost always 'No, but we know them.' We wonder. Could there be an assumption in there somewhere?

When we dig a little deeper it often emerges that the seller has confidence in only one of the four areas required to practise I Owe U.

I Owe U places demands on the seller. They need to prepare and research. They need to walk into a meeting with buyers equipped with:

■ knowledge of their buyer's preferred behaviours and personal style

■ knowledge of their own preferred behaviours and the impact this has on others

- knowledge of the buyer's business and market
- knowledge of their offering.

Salespeople get trained in the last point, but the first three they need to work out for themselves. That takes time and energy.

I Owe U is particularly challenging 'in the moment'. Many salespeople have their rehearsed lines and standard sales packs ready. But that does not make a good impression. What gives comfort to buyers is seeing salespeople perform in the moment – asking the right questions and making sound comments. By association, if you can think quickly and answer immediate questions, then you will be able to think quickly and fix bigger problems too.

The best salespeople – those with deep, long-term relationships based on trust – ask the tough questions about things that are outside their immediate area of expertise. They are prepared to step outside their own comfort zones in the interests of helping their buyers find answers to their key challenges.

Fortunately, help is available to target questions at the right areas. We have three approaches that can help sellers target the right areas – to uncover key challenges – and these are examined below:

- common areas for questioning
- Spicy Questions
- Value-Sheets.

6.10 Common areas for questioning

In following the SHAPE approach, **Surface**, **Hunt** and **Paint** questions typically revolve around five key business areas that we remember as 'Focus Five':

- Financial (revenue, profits, cashflow)
- Customers
- Competitors
- Market (market share, market perception)
- Employees

Look back at the examples of questions that we have been using and you will see that they tend to fit neatly into one of these five areas.

Once you have locked these areas into your head, formulating good questions and linking problems to consequences becomes much easier. In meetings, when a challenge is identified, referring to this mental checklist kick-starts the formulation of good **Hunt** and **Paint** questions.

6.11 Spicy Questions

We mentioned earlier that buyers sometimes feel that they are being interrogated when they get into a meeting with sellers. Equally, buyers sometimes need encouragement to move out of the detail and take a look at the bigger picture.

There are specific types of questions that help spice up the conversation with buyers, causing them to think deeply, or differently. Buyers enjoy the difference and sellers get a better quality of response.

No barriers

Gives the buyer permission to think about options with no barriers.

- 'Given unlimited time, money and resources what would the ideal situation be?'
- 'If you could change any aspect of the way your goods are transported, what would it be?'
- 'If you could locate your headquarters in any city, where would you choose?'
- 'If you were able to start over again, what kind of job would you do?'
- 'If cost was not an issue, what would be your preferred freight method?'

The key is to remove the normal barriers.

Positive/negative

Helps the buyer create a gap analysis by getting them to tell you what the best case and worst case scenarios are. Very useful early in a discussion as a way to surface key issues quickly.

- ▨ 'What are the three most important selection criteria? What are the three least important?'

- ▨ 'In which three areas do you think you lead your competitors? In which three areas do you think you might be behind?'

- ▨ 'What three things do you like best about your job? What are the three things you would change?'

The key to a good positive/negative question is to ask the positive first. Starting with the positive relaxes the buyer as they are talking about things that make them feel good. This wins 'permission' to ask the negative. Note also that we ask for three. Asking for one, or leaving the question open, gives the buyer the opportunity to give 'top-of-head' responses. Asking for three encourages them to think more deeply and gives the seller more and richer information to work with.

Non-stick

Relates a story from a third party, allowing the buyer to refute or build upon the content. Excellent for asking about sensitive issues, without it being perceived as your question.

- ▨ 'I met someone at a dinner party recently who exports garments from China. He told me that they have a lot of problems with customs delays for goods exported to the US. Do you think this is a widespread issue for companies manufacturing in China?'

- ▨ 'There has been a lot of talk in the trade press in recent months about the customs authorities in various countries getting tough on the under-declaration of value. Do you think this is an issue in Asia?'

- ▨ 'I read in the newspaper a couple of months ago that retaining quality staff is still a big issue for many companies. Is that something you see in your industry?'

Non-stick questions work in three stages. Start broad (the source), narrow to the issue, then go broad again (industry, market or geographical area). Poorly executed non-stick questions end by saying something like, 'Have *you* seen that,' or 'Is that an issue for *you*.' That is not non-stick!

Timeline

Gives the buyer a timeframe which can help them think about what is possible.

■ 'What major changes do you see happening [in your area] over the next three years?'

■ 'Tell me about the three most satisfying achievements of the last year. How about the three biggest challenges for next year?'

■ 'What is your vision for where this company will be in three years' time?'

■ 'What would you like to be doing three years from now?'

Break the pattern

Remove one step out of the normal process the buyer uses. This forces them to think outside the norm.

■ 'I know it does not sound plausible, but what would you do if all phones were out of order for one year, including mobiles?'

■ 'If the internet suddenly crashed for six months what options would you have?'

■ 'If all your staff resigned tomorrow and did not come back – what would you do?'

■ 'If fuel suddenly increased in price by 500% and motor vehicles were banned for a year, what would you do?'

Knock-down

Says something which is unrealistic that you are happy for the buyer to 'knock down' but which might change their thinking.

■ 'Do you think you could get 100% customer satisfaction?'

■ 'Is a 40% growth in profits feasible this year?'

■ 'Could you reduce your cost base by 50% over the next three years?'

One key point about a knock-down: you should not defend it when the buyer knocks it down. If you do then it is not a knock-down – it is something you believe.

All of these approaches work well and inject variety into the conversation. The skill lies in knowing which question to ask at what point in the discussion.

Facts and feelings

A final tip when it comes to questioning. You will have found out earlier, when considering the Octagon™ (Chapter 2), that you have a tendency to look at things from the perspective of facts or feelings. This will have an impact on the type of question you like to use.

Below are a few examples of facts and feelings questions.

Facts questions

■ 'How many consignments do you ship to Europe each month?'

■ 'What is the average shipment time?'

■ 'How much do you spend each year on shipping?'

■ 'How many people are employed to manage shipment and delivery?'

■ 'Have your customers experienced any loss of income as a result of delayed shipments?'

Facts questions tend to be useful at the **Surface** and **Engage** stage of the questioning process. Very useful when you are trying to get your head around an idea and also when you are trying to confirm some facts or next actions.

Feelings questions

■ 'How do you feel about the impact on market share?'

■ 'How do your staff feel about the down time?'

■ 'How much will it help you personally if this is achieved?'

■ 'How have employees reacted to having to work additional hours to clear the backlog?'

Feelings questions can be particularly useful when judging the importance of the issue to the buyer, i.e. around the **Hunt**, **Adjust** and **Paint** stages of the process.

The two types of question dictate a different type of response and so change the pace and energy.

Facts questions tend to be more direct and driven, and therefore the pace of discovery feels faster. In extreme, the process can feel like an interrogation to the buyer. Almost like you are driving a car with a manual gear system and you have forgotten to change up the gears so the engine is screaming. For example:

■ 'What is your profit?'

■ 'How does that compare to last year?'

■ 'Is that worse than you thought it would be?'

■ 'How do you plan to change things?'

■ 'When will you do that?'

■ 'How will you do that?'

Feelings questions are usually broader and drive some reflection rather than some action. In extreme it can feel to the buyer as if the conversation is going round in circles and not moving towards an aim. Again, using the manual car analogy, this is almost as if you have changed up the gears too soon and the engine is about to stall. For example:

■ 'How do you feel about the level of profit?'

■ 'What is your feeling about the difference between last year's and this year's profits?'

■ 'Do you worry about how people feel about your role in this?'

■ 'How do you feel about the impact you have made on the situation?'

■ 'How would increasing profits make you feel?'

■ 'How would implementing the changes immediately affect your feelings on this?'

Both types of question have their use, the key is to be aware of what type of questions you are asking and to mix them according to what you are trying to achieve at that stage in the conversation.

6.12 Value-Sheets

For some salespeople and buyers, structure is important. Think back to the Octagon™. Did you score high or low in the Free flowing/Organised behaviour category?

Knowing where to start the discussion; understanding the links between what a problem is and why it is a problem now when it wasn't before; what the value is in solving it. For such people, Value-Sheets are an extremely useful tool. For everyone else they are merely very useful!

Properly used, Value-Sheets continue to give credence to the salesperson as a clear listener and a clear thinker. Part of the success of the Value-Sheet is attributable to the clarity and simplicity of the process, part is due to the fact that it is a shared development process.

The process typically starts with a blank sheet of A4 paper in landscape. As part of the I Owe U start to the meeting, or at some other appropriate time in the meeting, the buyer is asked if they are OK with us, the sellers, documenting the discussion on a single sheet of paper. Buyers seldom refuse. Why would they?

Four column headings are then written on the paper and SHAPE questioning is used to populate the sheet:

Issue or challenge	Current situation	Desired future position	Value
Staff turnover.	31%. Morale low. No real culture.	Best in industry. The place to be.	Immeasurable.
Time to get product to market.	17 days. 20% rotten stock, unhappy customers, profitability dropping.	The best quality when it reaches store.	Profitability up 100%, demand-driven supply chain.

At all stages, the buyer should see what is being written. It is their thoughts and yours that are being recorded.

The value column records the value to the buyer of moving from the current situation to the desired future position. This may be numerical or emotive. If, for example, you ask, 'How important would it be for you to achieve the desired position?' and the buyer says, 'It would be good,' this is not sufficiently emotive. That means that the **Hunt** or **Paint** questions have not penetrated the buyer's thinking sufficiently, or that particular issue is not that important. Time to **Adjust**.

In terms of matching to SHAPE questions:

- You complete the *Issue or challenge* column through **Hunt** questions.
- You complete the *Current situation* column through **Surface** or **Hunt** questions.
- You complete the *Desired future position* column through **Paint** questions.
- You complete the *Value* column through **Adjust**, **Paint**, and **Engage** questions.

Sometimes we get asked why there is no 'Solution' column on the Value-Sheet. That is deliberate. A fifth column may be added during the process, more often it isn't. In part this is a recognition that there is rarely one sol-ution specific to one issue. The main reason, however, is that leaving out the solution sends a strong message to the buyer that the key purpose of the discussion is to help buyer and seller develop a clear, joint under-standing of the issues involved and the value of resolving them. Leaving out solutions also helps prevent the seller from falling into the trap of pushing their offering too early!

Award for bravery

The bravest use we have seen of the Value-Sheet was a client of ours who wanted to run a business lunch for a number of senior executives from different companies all in the same industry. Our client had no previous exposure to these companies or individuals who were all potential buyers.

They had the lunch and when the food was finished the chairperson asked everyone to turn over their placemats and on the back of each one was a blank Value-Sheet. There then ensued some vibrant one-on-one conversations around the table between our client's people and the executives from the other companies.

At the end of the meeting our client was asked to host a similar meeting every month.

Not bad from a standing start.

Completing a Value-Sheet is not a form-filling exercise. What is written mirrors the thought process and discussion.

One word of warning. Resist the temptation to partially complete a Value-Sheet before you get to the meeting. This is not co-development. By doing that you are saying, 'I am not listening, I know your issues and am pretty sure that I know the solution as well.' Don't do it.

In any one meeting we would suggest that you do not try to cover more than three issues. Cramming in too much content leads to issues not being covered in sufficient depth to identify needs properly.

One of the keys to success is continuing the process. At the end of the meeting photocopy the document and give the buyer a copy. This helps them to continue thinking about the topics discussed. If you are running a meeting of several people then you may want to complete the Value-Sheet on an electronic whiteboard. This is more visible and public, can be amended easily and printed immediately at the end of the meeting.

When you get back to your office word-process a 'finished' version. You should not add or change anything. This is just a smartened version that you will email to the buyer the same day – preferably with your organisation's name prominently included. We know of many situations where the Value-Sheet becomes the buyer organisation's internal reference document for discussing the issues, so you want your name on it!

At the end of your covering email you can say that you will call them tomorrow to make sure you have got everything right and to see if they have had any further thoughts. This keeps the collaboration moving forward.

In this chapter, we've introduced the core questioning approaches that lift I Owe U above other consultative sales approaches which involve elements of manipulation. In the next chapter, we introduce a further level of sophistication – a strategic enquiry approach that works very well in addressing key business challenges and engaging senior executives' interest.

Integrated Architects Ltd – part 2

Richard called Chris Schumacher of Integrated Architects and was surprised that Chris seemed to have forgotten most points from their meeting. Chris explained that it was one of many meetings on the same issue with a number of vendors all competing, and the meetings were all pretty much the same.

Richard was relieved when Chris agreed to one more half-hour meeting and he immediately called Emily to plan their approach.

At the meeting Richard asked if it was OK if they make some notes so that they could send a record of the conversation to Chris afterwards. Chris readily agreed and Emily explained that FuturePerfect like to use a technique involving the customer to record key meeting points – especially the points the customer makes. She put a sheet of paper into the middle of the table and wrote four headings.

Richard stuck pretty close to SHAPE, while Emily completed the Value-Sheet – occasionally asking Chris for clarification when she had not fully understood his reasoning.

Surprisingly, the meeting continued well over the half-hour that had been timetabled, and revealed two important challenges that Chris faced – neither of which Richard or Emily could immediately help with. One was the fact that their Finance Director had resigned recently and he was worried that others in the finance department may follow, which could have serious implications for billing and cashflow. The other was that he had heard that a competitor was about to reduce their fee rates by 15% and Chris was not sure as to how Integrated Architects should respond.

Although they did not have answers to the issues, Richard said that he would talk to a friend of his who worked for an executive recruitment firm to see if he had any ideas. Emily promised to have a think about any other buyers of FuturePerfect who have faced competitor price-cutting and see if she could get them to contact Chris to compare notes.

After an hour they had barely started to talk about the one issue that Richard and Emily could help with. At this point, Chris apologised and said he needed to go to another meeting, but he also said that he was pleased they had come back to see him again. He said he would get his secretary to line up another meeting to continue their discussions.

Key messages

▨ Avoid assumptions.

▨ Stay in step with the buyer, responding to their moves – as opposed to taking control and forcing the pace.

▨ SHAPE the process to ensure you arrive at a solid, shared understanding of prioritised needs.

▨ Surface – to elicit facts.

Hunt – to understand the challenges/problems behind the facts.

Adjust – to ask permission, confirm priority or change direction.

Paint – the outcomes/benefits of taking action.

Engage – agree next steps.

▨ Ease your way into SHAPE by memorising key drivers of concern and adding variety through the use of 'Spicy' Questions.

■ Use Value-Sheets to display structure, understanding and a desire to deliver value.

■ Always retain a 'helping' mindset to assist the buyer in articulating their needs.

7

Moving to a higher level

'A problem cannot be solved at the same level of thinking as that
which created it.'

Albert Einstein, Physicist and Thinker (1879–1955)

I Owe U salespeople strive to engage buyers at a strategic level as
opposed to a tactical level. In this chapter we help those who favour a strategic approach to uncover the key drivers behind the immediate issues.

Bear Toys Ltd – part 1

Richard and Emily had heard rumours that Bear Toys were not happy
with their current accounting system. It apparently did not provide all
the functions that their CEO, Madeleine Mater, needed as an
increasingly significant part of the business was being driven by
exports.

Thanks to a reference from a contact in the company, Richard and
Emily got a meeting with Madeleine.

They followed the SHAPE process, asked some great questions and it
quickly became clear that the rumours were true. Madeleine was
looking for a new accounting system.

Madeleine was very keen to talk about the system and find out what
Richard and Emily's offering could do. It appeared to be a match
made in heaven. They got on really well and their solution appeared
genuinely to fit Madeleine's needs.

Madeleine moved on to cost and after a brief negotiation they agreed
a 7% discount.

▶

> The next morning Richard was somewhat surprised to get a phone call from his contact saying that although Madeleine had bought the accounting system from FuturePerfect, he was aware that she was talking to a competitor of Richard's about buying a new inventory management system.

The skills covered in this chapter will not be applicable in all situations but in the right one they are incredibly powerful – especially with senior executives such as chief executive officers (CEOs), chief finance officers (CFOs) and chief operations officers (COOs). The aim is to get buyers thinking at a higher level.

7.1 Different levels of conversation

If you are selling widgets to a procurement department then the thinking skills we discuss below will have relatively little immediate benefit. However the higher up the buyer food chain you are trying to sell and the more complex the offering you are selling, the more important these skills become.

Let's try an example to explain the concept. If you walked into the bathroom and noticed that, as usual, one of the taps was dripping, what would your mental reaction be? The reaction to this situation indicates the level of thinking you naturally fall into. Which of the following is closest to your reaction?

- Level 1 – I need to turn the tap tighter.
- Level 2 – We must put new washers in the taps in this bathroom.
- Level 3 – We need a new bathroom.

    . . .

- Level 8 – Water – now that's an interesting concept!

Clearly there is a big gap between levels 3 and 8 but hopefully this makes the point.

There is a high likelihood that the higher you scored in the Big picture/ Detail category in the Octagon™ (see Chapter 2) the closer you are to level

8, or at least level 3, and the easier you will find it to elevate your thinking and your conversations.

Albert Einstein used a lot of these processes to arrive at some of his greatest concepts and ideas. Much of the recent work in this area was carried out by Elliott Jacques, a leading psychologist and a pioneer in human development theory (see the website of the Requisite Organisation International Institute, www.requisite.org). He talked about eight levels of thinking. We have simplified Jacques' eight levels to four (level 8 equates to level 4 in our structure).

Jacques hypothesised that an individual's value to an organisation was determined to a large extent by the length of their horizon. That is to say that the further a person can look into the future and the bigger the picture they can see, the more they will be able to help the organisation as they move up the leadership hierarchy. Ultimately the CEO needs to have the biggest thinking and longest vision.

There are three reasons why this may matter to you, the salesperson:

▦ You need to be able to match the thinking levels of senior buyers in order to develop better rapport.

▦ You want to help take the buyer out of the detail to paint the overall picture and the value of a solution. This could make it easier to sell your offering.

▦ You want to help the buyer solve some of their problems but at present they can only see the symptoms and not the cause. This could really help you deepen the relationship as you are helping them address the real issue.

We call this process the Fitting Concept because it is about making the details fit the overall aim.

Keith is in the process of building a house. He and his wife needed to decide who will build the house. At the end of the day there are a lot of builders and they all build good, impressive, solid houses.

Keith was interested in the overall concept. Open planned, breezes,

▶

verandas etc. His wife wanted to talk about the colour of the roof, where the cooker would go and what shape the stairs would be.

The builder chosen managed to move his conversation between the levels and also managed to use level 4 thinking to help point out some possible problems with some of the detailed ideas.

For instance Keith's wife wanted the lounge a specific shape which she had seen in a magazine. The builder pointed out that he could do that, but it would have a huge impact on the overall feel of the house and it would make wrap-around verandas, a key part of the open feel, almost impossible.

He could have agreed with the shape of the lounge and built the house to the specific details wanted, but Keith and his wife would have resented him in the long run because the overall impact of the house would not have been what they wanted.

By doing this he built a relationship with both Keith and his wife, and did this by not always agreeing with both of them but by showing he wanted to help them build the house they dreamed of.

Keith and his wife moved their thinking from believing all builders were the same to being nervous that this builder may be too busy to build their house.

Below is a table which will give you a better idea of how this manifests in different situations:

	General	House building	Running a business
Level 1	Fittings, details, specifics, individual, day.	Appliances	Shorter working hours, profit margin.
Level 2	Situation, actions, team, month.	Size of lounge	Work–life balance, annual profit.
Level 3	Overall plan, strategy, achievements, department, year.	Number of floors	Integrating work and family, long-term profit projection.
Level 4	Concepts, dreams, vision, organisation, legacy.	Space and light	A place where people want to be, sustainability of the business.

This may all sound very simple and logical, but for many people applying the skill is very hard.

You can go through the levels in any sequence with your buyer, and to a large extent the sequence will depend upon the personality of the buyer. If they are a detailed buyer then you should not start at level 4 as they are likely to respond, mentally if not verbally, with 'I don't believe you,' or 'prove it' or 'be realistic'.

If you are dealing with a big picture buyer then to start at level 1 and then work through levels 2 and 3 before getting to level 4 may feel tedious to them.

You need to be prepared to flex your approach.

7.2 Getting from level 1 to level 4

If you do not know the personality of your buyer, or if you deal with multiple buyers at the same time, then it is very difficult to get the sequence correct. If you are dealing with extreme big picture buyers then we would suggest you start at level 4 and work backwards through levels 3 then 2 then 1. If however you are dealing with very detailed buyers then you will start at level 1 and may never get past level 2.

A compromise order that works well in many situations is as follows:

▪ Start at level 1 – this allows the buyer to discuss all the current things that they see as being good and bad with the given situation.

▪ Move to level 4 – this pushes the buyer away from the negativity that may come at the level 1 stage. This is where you move to the positive future, painting a picture of where the dream lies. You can stop at this level, and that will satisfy the level 4 thinkers, but you will not have moved to action.

▪ Then to level 3 – this helps the buyer focus on the key things that need to be achieved in order to be able to make sure that the level 4 goals are achieved. These are not action points. Take the house building example. It may be that level 3 is that the house needs to be two storeys high. That is not an action point – just something that needs to be achieved.

▪ Finish with level 2 – these are the actions that need to be taken in order to ensure that level 3 is achieved. For the house example it may be that we need to dig deeper foundations for a two-storey house. At this stage it is likely that some of the actions address some of the level 1 issues raised earlier in the process. It is however likely that some of the issues raised at the level 1 stage do not get addressed. That is fine because if the process has worked effectively the buyer will see that those issues, whilst they seem important, are in reality not key to the achievement of the vision.

The 'hardest' part of the process for many people is moving from level 1 to level 4. The skill in moving them involves asking the right question.

In Chapter 6 we looked at the SHAPE questioning process. To move from level 1 to level 4 thinking you are looking to ask Paint questions (covered in section 6.6), and particularly powerful ones at that.

You may also need to use some of the techniques mentioned in section 6.11 to help buyers move beyond their mental road-blocks and move to a higher level of thinking.

Advo, a professional services firm that Keith was working with, had a client, RealTop, an estate agency. The relationship was however a technical relationship (see section 3.1).

Advo wanted to sell RealTop a solution to a problem that they faced. Keith was asked to help Advo sell the new solution. In the planning stage it became apparent to Keith that there may be an opportunity not only to sell this solution, but to focus on improving Advo's relationship with RealTop and also possibly sell a much better solution to a much bigger problem.

The CFO and COO of RealTop came to a meeting that Keith ran for Advo. The meeting was set around a boardroom table with a whiteboard.

After the usual preliminaries RealTop was more than happy to talk about the current situation, good and bad. This was noted on the whiteboard, taking approximately 20 minutes.

Keith explained that before deciding on solutions, they should make sure that these would be in line with RealTop's vision for the company. RealTop were happy to hear this, if maybe a little mystified as to what was going to happen next.

Keith asked the question, 'What is the "dream" for RealTop?' and got the usual response: 'To be the biggest estate agency in the country.' Now, that may be a vision, but it is not particularly engaging.

He then asked the question, 'What is it that you do?' Answer: 'We sell houses. . . and apartments.'

▶

The next question was the key: 'What is it that enables you to sell houses and apartments?'

There was then a silence of about 30 seconds. This was clearly not something that RealTop had ever really thought about. They could not answer the question: they did not know.

Keith then reversed the question: 'What would it be that, if your competitors had it, would enable them to kill you in the market?'

That answer came quite quickly: 'To have a reputation for being trusted.'

So the level 4 for RealTop became: *To have a reputation for being trusted*. A stretch goal maybe, but nonetheless a very engaging dream.

Keith then worked on the level 3. RealTop said that it was their franchisees who dictated who were recruited as salespeople, and the salespeople were the 'front' of the organisation. Franchisees were typically salespeople. This meant that there was a high possibility that most franchisees were recruiting, training and rewarding salespeople based on the franchisees' view of a good salesperson – which might be different to RealTop's ideas. The level 3 became: *To have franchisees who are well-rounded 'people and business' people*.

Keith had to stop the meeting at that stage. Enough progress had been made. Moving to actions at this stage would have been premature. RealTop needed time to reflect on the discussions.

The whole atmosphere in the room had changed. In a very short space of time the way that Advo was viewed by RealTop changed. It evolved from technical to partner. Here was someone who was really trying to help them succeed – not by selling their solution, but by trying to help them see their dream and then figure out a way to help them achieve it.

The meeting reconvened the following week and a level 2 action plan was developed to support the need for franchisees to be 'people and business' people. The level 2 plan was to assess the behaviours of successful and unsuccessful franchisees (determined by market share); then to define the behaviours of successful franchisees and change the recruitment criteria accordingly; and finally, to run training sessions to help those already in place make the changes they needed to make.

RealTop also bought the initial solution that Advo wanted to sell them without even going to proposal; possibly because Advo was now viewed as a trusted business partner.

There are a few points to bear in mind in order to make this approach work.

In much the same way as we mention in Chapter 6, you cannot assume what the buyer's level 4 will be. It has to be their dream. Your role is to ask the questions that help them to new levels of thinking.

Below is an example level 1 and level 4 for a hypothetical company, Logistics Limited. Now, imagine you are the salesperson of a computer network company attempting to sell Logistics an enhancement to their system which would enable them to connect their tracking system to that of companies to whom they sometimes outsource work.

Imagine you have decided that you would like to have a broader conversation about their business goals, to see if there are other ways in which you can help. Think about other questions you could ask to get the buyer from level 1 to level 4. One question is included on the form below to get you started. See if you can think of two more.

Name of buyer company	Logistics Ltd	Name of individual buyer	Mary Pearce
Level 1 issues	Logistics company that ships goods globally. Number 2 in most markets. Good brand. Outsourced in some small countries. 93,000 employees. Web site. One global tracking system for own company. Not linked to outsourced companies.		
Possible questions to create level 4	a If you saw your company on the front page of Global Business magazine, what would you like the heading to say?		
	b		
	c		
Level 4	A company that is seen by the market place as entirely web driven with a one-stop shop web site for clients, staff and outsource companies for marketing, pricing, buying, selling, space sharing, tracking and feedback.		

The questions you would ask above are significantly different to the ones you would ask in order to sell only a system enhancement. Some level 4 questions we would ask are:

▨ If you were a buyer of yours, how would you describe the ideal logistics company?

▨ What would the 'perfectly efficient' logistics company look like?

▨ If you had to downsize your workforce by 50% what would you do to become even more efficient and effective?

Now think of a situation closer to home. You might have a suitable buyer in your portfolio on whom you could try this process. Alternatively, think of a potential buyer with whom you have no relationship. Now consider the individual or potential buyer. Think of some questions you could ask in order to get the buyer to tell you their level 4 'dreams'.

Remember, you cannot presume to know what their dream is, but for this exercise we can think of some possible high-level conceptual situations for your buyer. Now think whether the questions you thought of asking would solicit these conceptual ideas from the buyer. If not then try again to think of questions that will solicit the types of level 4 responses you are hoping to get.

If you would like to write all this down and actually start planning, you can use the planning form in Appendix 4.

Once you have the level 4 for your buyer there is still a temptation to go straight to action points, i.e. level 2, rather than level 3. That can work, but there is a risk that there is too big a gap between the two levels for people to make the link and the reason 'why' they are taking a specific action may be missed.

Following through with the example of the one-stop shop, web-based level 4 for the logistics company, we give below some possible level 3 ideas and then some level 2 actions.

Level 3 – Achievements:

▨ Understand what networks we and the outsource companies have globally

▨ Understand what the next generation of web development may offer

▨ Know what buyers really want in terms of accessibility to technology and people.

Level 2 – Actions:

- ▨ Identify the companies to whom work has been outsourced
- ▨ Contact the technology departments of all outsourced companies
- ▨ Contact some leading people on web development
- ▨ Write a report on the future of the web
- ▨ Survey to current buyers on their needs.

You now not only have a better understanding of the rationale behind, and the theory of, elevating the conversation but you may also have some specific plans regarding questions you can ask one of your buyers.

In the next chapter we discuss what you should do at the end of the meeting and afterwards to cement what has been discussed and agreed.

Bear Toys Ltd – part 2

On the back of the success of their first meeting with Madeleine Mater, CEO of Bear Toys, Richard and Emily managed to get another meeting. This time though they decided on a different approach.

Very early in the meeting Madeleine asked if FuturePerfect's Inventory Manager software would serve her needs. Resisting the temptation to say 'Yes', Emily responded by saying that it would, but she wondered whether, since they had just bought a new accounting system and were now looking at an inventory management system, there may be bigger technology issues. Emily asked permission to ask a few questions about the current situation with regard to Bear Toys' overall use of technology.

Madeleine informed them that they had different systems for each of their four operations – human resources, business development, accounting and inventory management. She also mentioned that as the company was opening international offices they were replicating this model overseas. Some of these systems were good, some not.

Emily asked, 'If you were to raise your profit margin per customer by 50% what would your technology have to look like?'

It took Madeleine a little time to gather her thoughts and even then all she could say was that she had never really thought of technology as a way of raising profit margin. She had always thought technology was more about individual department efficiency.

▶

After further thought she said that it would make sense if all the systems were the best at what they were trying to do, were all connected, had one access point and were available on a global expanding basis.

The conversation level had changed completely.

Madeleine asked if this were possible. Richard responded that it may well be possible, but there were a few things they would need to ascertain first:

- Richard and Emily would need understand Bear Toys' operations and value chain so they could see where technology might be used.
- They would need to understand Madeleine's vision for the company and her strategy to get there.
- They would need to know all the current systems that were being used.
- They would need to look at what was the best that was being currently used around the world.

Only once they knew this would they be able to answer Madeleine's question. Madeleine was very happy to hear that someone was trying to help her achieve her vision for the business. They then all worked together to draw up an action plan to be able to find out the answers to all the above.

Richard and Emily did not leave with a contract, but they did leave with a big thank you from Madeleine.

A couple of days later Richard's friend called to say he had heard that Madeleine had cut off discussions with all other technology suppliers until Richard and Emily had completed their review.

Key messages

- Understand the value of moving conversations to the 'big picture'.
- Recognise that thinking occurs at different 'levels'.
- Understand your own natural thinking level and flex this to match your buyer's preferred level.
- Move from level 1 to level 4 by using unblocking Paint questions or Spicy Questions.
- Don't move to action points too soon in the process.

8

Cementing credibility and trust

'No-one wants advice, only collaboration.'

John Steinbeck, Author (1902–1968)

In this chapter we look at how to make sure that you keep in contact with the buyer and continuously maintain or improve the level of trust.

Neal and Danube Computers Ltd – part 1

Richard and Emily had a meeting with Neal, head of technical development at Danube Computers Ltd. Neal had expressed interest in FuturePerfect helping them with the technical development of some of their own machines.

The meeting went very well and Neal said he would call Emily in a few days with the decision.

A week passed and still no contact from Neal, so Emily decided to initiate the call. Neal's secretary answered the phone and explained that Neal had been called to New York for an urgent meeting, so would not be able to call Emily as planned. He has asked that they submit a detailed proposal for how they would provide technical assistance based on the discussions in their previous meeting.

Emily told Richard that they needed to start work immediately as this type of proposal normally took two weeks to complete and involved all the departments in the company.

A week later Emily was feeling very happy at the progress on the proposal – it would have taken only a couple more days to finish. But, before it was finished, Neal called wanting to clarify some of the points he had made in the original meeting.

It appeared that either something had changed at Danube or Emily had misheard Neal. Either way the proposal would need to be revised.

8.1 Confirming the situation

Lawyers are smart people. After meeting with a client, many have developed the habit of quickly recording the key points discussed and reflecting this back to their clients in letter form. This simple action is incredibly effective. Here's why. This device, which we call a CC letter has multiple benefits:

■ It demonstrates responsiveness and respect – showing that you have listened and that you are interested in what the buyer said.

■ It is collaborative – inviting the buyer to continue the dialogue begun in the meeting.

■ It helps avoid misunderstandings – especially important when working across languages or cultures.

■ It serves as a reminder of what was said when you return later with clouded memories.

■ It becomes the reference within the buyer's organisation for discussions on that topic.

All this from a simple record of the points discussed at the meeting. Absolutely!

The CC letter was first introduced to us by Ken Everett, a special friend, who helped David co-develop a relationship sales training programme. David has never forgotten his first use of this tool.

It was during his first month in Hong Kong. David had recently arrived from the UK, in a new place, with a new employer, working in Learning and Development.

▶

Tasked with talking to the head of one of the business divisions about training for his 300+ employees, he set out to meet him with some trepidation. This man, we'll call him John Smith, had a fearsome reputation. He had a quick temper and let people know exactly what he thought when their performance did not meet his exacting standards. He also disliked David's boss.

They had a cordial meeting. David asked lots of questions and he was very open about the challenges he faced and the many ways in which he felt that the Learning and Development team were failing to provide the help John's people needed. After the meeting, David returned to his office and quickly wrote a CC letter, in email format, and sent it off.

The next morning David was instructing a workshop. At morning coffee break, he checked the message board and feared the worst. Three words: 'Call John Smith'. What, he wondered, had he said that had upset John? With some anxiety, he dialled the number. John answered straight away.

'Ah David,' he said 'thanks for calling back. I just wanted to tell you that it's good to know that finally there is someone in Learning and Development who actually listens.'

You could have knocked David over with a feather. He became a convert there and then, and he's been an advocate ever since.

So, what does a CC letter look like? Here is the format:

Dear Customer,

(Thank)

Thank you for meeting with us to discuss. . . or
I enjoyed our meeting yesterday and the discussion . . . or
Thank you for sparing the time to meet with me yesterday, I hope you found the discussion as useful as I did. . .

(Clarify understanding)

I thought it would be helpful if I set out my understanding of the points we discussed yesterday. . . or
We covered many points yesterday and I thought it would be helpful

to note down what I heard so that we make sure we both go forward with the same shared understanding. . .

My understanding:

■ First point, either in order discussed or order of importance (most important first). Where possible, describe the challenge discussed, then the consequences of doing nothing or of solving it (cost/benefit)

■ Second point . . .

■ Third point . . .

Please let me know if I have understood your comments correctly or if you have other thoughts to add. . . or

I hope I've remembered everything of importance, but do please let me know if I have missed or misunderstood any of the points we discussed, or if you have had further thoughts.

(Confirm next steps)

We agreed that the next steps would be . . . or
We agreed that I would get back to you with . . . or
In terms of next steps, you agreed to provide more information on xxxxxx and I said I would xxxxxxxxx.
I will call you next week to give you an update on progress.

Yours sincerely,

Note the three key stages in the letter:

■ Thank

■ Clarify understanding

■ Confirm next steps.

Other key rules for CC letters are:

■ The tone should be informal and littered with phrases such as 'you said', 'we discussed', 'you explained', 'we agreed'.

■ Try not to mention whatever it is that you are selling, and if you must – because you discussed it at the meeting – do it towards the end.

■ Respond quickly because a CC letter's enormous value degrades rapidly over time. If you meet in the morning, try to send the CC letter by the end of the same day or the next morning at the latest. By the end of the day following, you've lost a high percentage of the value.

■ It should be short, not more than two pages.

Another powerful thing about CC letters is that they are easy to write. Written mostly in bullet point format, they are quick, informal and forgiving of linguistic and grammatical errors. Moreover, for most meetings, we all know that we should write notes of meeting – typically for our own reference or for risk management purposes. It takes only a little effort to transform meeting notes to a CC letter. Actually, what works better is to write a CC letter first, then omit the top and tail to arrive at a less formal than usual, but still acceptable, meeting record.

In training workshops, we ask participants to hold a mock meeting and then, in groups, to write a CC letter based on the meeting. We then ask each group to read out their letters. The other groups give feedback based on:

■ Does it sound like we are 'helping' or 'selling'?

■ Does it sound collaborative – are we doing it 'with them' or 'to them'?

■ Does it sound informal or formal?

There are always wide variations and when the letters are read out the impact is immediately apparent. The main things to watch out for are:

■ Use of 'you' versus 'me', 'I' or 'we' (where 'we' means you and your organisation). The more we talk about ourselves, the more we put distance between ourselves and the buyer – the more it sounds like we are doing it to them rather than with them

■ Mention of your offering. It's striking that as soon as the letter mentions this, the tone seems to change and become more pushy, less collaborative. This does not mean that you cannot mention your offering – it just means that you need to be very careful how you mention it.

■ Next steps. Is the commitment to move forward a shared one – or are you, the vendor, doing all the work? In a collaborative relationship, both parties have responsibilities. If all the steps are on your side, try to ask for something from the other party – if only to test their level of commitment. Typically, we ask for some information from them that will help us put together a better response. If they are not willing to provide information, it is a fairly sure sign that they are not committed.

To give an idea of how a completed CC letter looks, and the sort of response it generates, we've included an actual exchange of emails below, with the names omitted to protect those involved.

Seller's initial email

Date: Today, 09:42
From: Seller
To: Buyer

Subject: Our meeting

Dear Buyer,

TRAINING NEEDS

Thank you for taking the time to meet us yesterday afternoon. We were very interested to hear the change management plans for AllOfYou.

I thought it might be helpful if I confirmed our understanding of the key points we discussed, so that going forward, we are both thinking in the same direction.

My understanding:
* You explained the restructuring of AllOfYou and that you are undertaking change management work with our AAA team.
* In discussing the changes you described the need for consistent processes as well as a mindset change. You also described how your different work units have historically worked separately, whereas in the new environment individuals from each unit will need to work together as part of larger project teams. You said that the current silo mentality could not carry over to the new project teams as this would severely affect the teams' productivity.
* We discussed the various challenges you are facing and we shared our view that your situation is quite similar to that of many

other government and quasi-government bodies that we have been working with. We also explained how we work closely with our AAA team, assisting them in their change assignments where formal classroom training is required.

*   You outlined how any training programme would need to be integrated into a broader change programme and we outlined a number of different activities that could be undertaken before and after any training event to ensure effectiveness. We also talked specifically about 'action learning', where a specialist coach is made available to work alongside a team throughout a specific assignment. The benefit of such a coach is that they help the team learn through pragmatic on-the-job interventions.

*   Specifically on project management, we introduced our project management methodology and talked through the workbook, highlighting that the programme may be customised for specific organisations – principally through adapting case studies. You mentioned that a large part of the instruction would need to be in the local language and we confirmed that this would not be a problem.

I hope I've remembered everything, but please let me know if I've missed anything, or if you have further points to add.

<u>Next steps</u>

*   In terms of next steps, you said that you were planning on running a senior management workshop to accomplish two main objectives:

    1. mindset change
    2. process change.

*   You will look at the strategy going forward and talk to AAA's team about the training element.
*   We will also speak to AAA about their work with you.

*   I will send through an overview of the Project
    Management course (please see attached file).

Thank you again for your time and we look forward
to hearing from you.

Kind regards

Seller

Buyer's response

Date: Today, 18:38
To: Seller
From: Buyer

Subject: RE: TRAINING NEEDS

Dear Seller,

Thank you again for the time you spent with us and
the ideas offered.

As said, I am rethinking a number of approaches to
this matter of changing the culture of AllOfYou,
which have to deal with the process itself in
order to be effective. But in terms of the overall
plan and the timing and of course the cost of
running some of those programmes we talked about,
xxx and I are still working very hard on the
specifics. Once we have more details, we shall be
speaking to both you and the AAA team.

Thank you so much for capturing all that we had
talked about yesterday – which helps to put all
the many ideas and issues into perspective.

Thank you again and look forward to working with
you all.

Regards,

Buyer

The example above is a genuine example and is a typical response to receiving a CC letter.

'Thank you so much for capturing all that we had talked about yesterday – which helps to put all the many ideas and issues into perspective.'

Could you ask for a better response?

The CC letter is another important tool that enables the I Owe U practitioner to differentiate themselves from the pack.

8.2 No proposals

In Chapter 6 we introduced Value-Sheets as a mechanism for working with buyers to collaboratively develop approaches to their challenges. Collaboration is a core principle of the I Owe U approach. Solutions to challenges are worked out jointly between the seller and the buyer, with mutually beneficial goals. Proposals are often not needed or are a formality.

In the table below, we compare the characteristics of a traditional proposal versus an I Owe U approach (where any final details are discussed in a face-to-face meeting) or Value-Sheet. It makes a strong case for avoiding formal proposals.

I Owe U approach or Value-Sheet	*Traditional formal proposal*
Is exploratory	Is final
Highly customised	Relatively generic
Suggests options	Promotes a single solution
Asks for feedback	Asks for a decision
Solving	Selling
Conversational	Formal
Time efficient and easy to produce	Time consuming and difficult to produce

With I Owe U, the sales process progresses naturally and the aim is to avoid time-consuming and value-killing formal quotations and proposals.

Secure the work, then discuss the details

Many businesses develop standard terms and conditions to protect against generic business risks.

One of our clients was in the habit of including their standard terms as an appendix to their proposals. We persuaded them that this was not such a good idea as it was possible that one of the detailed conditions might be contentious to the buyer. Better to let them select you to provide the service first, then argue about the details. It will be harder for them to change once they have made the decision.

Interestingly, some months later, a different business unit of the same company lost a contract because they included details of their liability cap (in the event that they were sued) in a proposal and the buyer found this contentious, ultimately switching to a competitor for the provision of over US$1 million of business.

It is a knee-jerk reaction for many buyers to request a proposal. And why wouldn't they? It's not as if it requires much effort on their part other than reading the thing once it is produced. Worse still, many times we have seen vendors automatically offer to send through a proposal at the end of a meeting with a potential target. What is so amazing about this is that often the vendor has not even established whether the buyer needs the offering, but they fool themselves that by sending in a proposal, the buyer will somehow be persuaded. This approach is both 'pushy' and time consuming. Don't do it.

Proposals submitted ≠ business won

Some people even try to measure sales success by the number of proposals submitted. What a sham!

David once worked alongside a master of this forlorn tactic. Challenged on the performance of their business unit, this person would always quote the number of proposals that had been submitted that month. Amazingly, it took the organisation a considerable time to see through this smokescreen and realise that submitting proposals was no indicator of success.

The conversion rate of proposals to wins turned out to be incredibly low. The proposals submitted were generic, generally not requested, and had the effect of making the vendor appear unprofessional and desperate. Ultimately, the person behind the charade was dismissed and their entire business unit disbanded.

David has spent many years reviewing proposals and talking to buyers about them. He's learned many things in that time, but the saddest of all is that very few people read the proposals that are presented to them. Someone in the organisation will read them, but it is rarely the person making the decision. At best, if you're smart and you include an executive summary of no more than two pages, potential buyers are more likely to read that. Then they'll flick to the page on pricing.

Even highly-paid and highly-valued management consultants fall into the 'proposals trap'. We once attended a meeting with a senior consultant and as we left the meeting he commented, 'I guess you'll go away and write a proposal now.' 'No way', was our response.

We returned a week later to talk through our approach to the client's challenge and at the end of the meeting he asked us when we could start. We gave him a date and said that we should formally agree price and scope before we started. That formal discussion became a formality!

Once you realise that price is really what people are asking for when they ask for a proposal, it becomes much easier to challenge buyers and avoid wasting time on a process that adds minimal value.

Faced with a request for a proposal it is easy to politely probe whether this is really necessary. A conversation might go something like this:

Buyer: 'So can you put together a proposal please.'

Seller: 'Of course, can you give me an idea of what we should include?'

Buyer: 'Ermmm. . .well. Technical specifications, a project schedule, citations, details of team members.'

Seller: 'No problem. Will these details form the basis of the decision on which vendor you will use?'

Buyer: 'Not really, but it is standard practice.'

Seller: 'Well, I can let you have some standard documents that provide that sort of detail, but what I'd really like to do is provide the information you need to make your decision.'

Buyer: 'OK. If you can confirm what we've discussed and come back with a quotation, that should do for starters.'

This is an example of an actual conversation. Of course, not all situations are the same, and some organisations demand proposals. Our suggestion is to make sure you understand what information is important to the decision-making process and focus your energies appropriately.

The draft work-plan

Another option after an initial meeting with a client is a draft work-plan. This is particularly useful when the buyer has an urgent need. It should be sent to the buyer within a couple of days of the meeting and include all the key aspects of the first stages of a project – assuming you win the work.

It will not include the whole project, but will include suggestions for the next steps in the discovery process. A typical draft work-plan looks like this:

When	31 Aug	30 Sept	31 Oct	30 Nov
What	Interview all staff members	Produce report	Management workshop	Interview selected staff members
Who	Keith	Keith and David	David	Keith
Why	To identify what their concerns are	To inform the leadership team what the staff think	To agree the actions to be taken	To understand how the actions have been received by staff

This relatively informal type of proposal is useful because it can be produced quickly and it gives the buyer the key urgent and important information.

The draft work-plan approach will not work in all situations but we use it in about 40% of cases in order to reduce the need to provide a full and formal proposal.

In summary, our rules for proposals are:

▪ Start with a mindset that says: 'Formal proposals are time-consuming, add little or no value, and I don't want to do them unless I absolutely must.'

▪ If someone asks you to prepare a proposal, ask (politely) what information they need – then give it, verbally, and ask if they need it confirmed in writing. If they say yes – and much of the time they don't – write it in a simple letter. In our long experience what they really want to know is the price.

- Keep any proposal as short as possible – entire proposals often do not get read. You can differentiate your proposal by making it the shortest.

- Work with your buyers to generate whatever they need that you can help with, then confirm this with them using a CC letter that describes the next steps. Seek commitment to next steps as opposed to 'closing the sale'.

8.3 Proof

On occasion, when proposals are requested, it is not only about price – it's about comfort too. What do we mean by comfort? Well, we see two types of comfort:

First, comfort that your service or product will not disappoint. This need for reassurance increases where the value or impact of the offering increases, or where the buyer's experience of working with you or your organisation is limited.

Second, comfort that you will treat them well – that you respect them and have their best interests at heart. Also, if you're providing a service that involves them working with you, that they will enjoy that experience.

The best way to give the comfort buyers are looking for is to talk about your previous experience. Instead, the way that many organisations choose to give comfort is by saying how big they are, how many customers or clients they have, and by naming those customers. This is not proof – it's boasting – something that often works against the seller's efforts to persuade the buyer that they will enjoy working with the seller.

Alternatively, or additionally, organisations make grand statements about their 'commitment', the quality of their people, and the superior quality of their product or service. Again though, these statements are empty of any proof.

If you want to give real comfort to buyers, talk about previous actual incidents where your offering has been put to use. That is proof. Describe in some detail what happened, with or without mentioning the name of your customer or client.

For greater credibility, think about actually confessing to some difficulties you've faced with other buyers and how you overcame them. Many salespeople cannot bring themselves to criticise their offering or their organisation, which is a pity. No-one believes a perfect picture. Who would a buyer feel more comfortable with – someone who shields the truth behind a veneer of polished perfection, or someone who admits mistakes and knows how to fix them?

In this chapter we've looked at how to cement credibility with your buyers and how to avoid investing unnecessary time and energy in lengthy proposal processes. In the next chapter we look at how to make an impact in those situations where proposals and the presentations that tend to accompany them prove to be unavoidable.

Neal and Danube Computers Ltd – part 2

Emily recognised that it was better that Neal had called before FuturePerfect's proposal was finished, but she didn't want the same thing to happen a second time. She decided to send Neal a CC letter confirming their telephone conversation.

She spent 20 minutes typing it up and then emailed it to Neal with a covering note saying she would call the next day to make sure she had understood Neal properly. However, a few minutes later she got a call from Neal. Yes, it was a good summary and she had recorded their points accurately. In fact, on reading the email, Neal had an additional thought on training that he wanted to include.

At the end of the conversation Emily used an Engage question and Neal confirmed that yes, Emily should now start work on a full proposal.

Key points

- Use CC letters to confirm shared understanding and continue the collaborative process.

- Develop a mindset that avoids written proposals unless absolutely necessary.

- Provide proof of capability through sharing experience – both the good and the bad.

9

Presenting your ideas for positive impact

'In the modern world of business, it is useless to be a creative original thinker unless you can also sell what you create. Management cannot be expected to recognise a good idea unless it is presented to them by a good salesman.'

David Ogilvy, founder of Ogilvy & Mather

I Owe U salespeople do their best to secure work without the need for a formal presentation. However, where one is required they focus on presenting their ideas as concisely and memorably as possible. In this chapter we look at ways to do this.

Hotel Ltd – part 1

Richard and Emily had been in discussions with Hotel Ltd for six months and finally had been asked to make a pitch presentation to the board.

They wrote the script, developed the slides and rehearsed for hours. They were confident that they had everything perfect, and a great chance of impressing the buyer and winning the contract.

The presentation seemed to go well. There were only a couple of interruptions when someone wanted clarification. At the end they fielded a few hard questions. They had an answer for each one and gave them with great confidence, apart from the question on pricing, when Emily stumbled slightly and hinted that she may be able to reduce the price a bit.

A week passed and they received a phone call saying that the company was having trouble reaching a decision. They had the sense that Richard and Emily may have the best offering, but they could not

▶

remember exactly what it was that gave them that impression. In fact, they confessed, all the vendors' presentations had been quite similar and they couldn't recall whether some of the key points had been made by Richard and Emily or one of their competitors.

What they could remember, though, was that Emily had said that she could offer a discount. Consequently, they had decided to request FuturePerfect and one other vendor to make a second presentation.

There is a school of thought that says you can only lose at the presentation stage – you should have secured the sale in the run-up to any presentation. The presentation should be a formality; perhaps a way for the key buyer to give other influencers and interested parties an opportunity to get comfort that the right choice has been made.

Certainly, having sat on both sides of the table, it's fair to say that more business is lost as a result of poor presentations than is won as a result of good ones.

The key to continuing to make a good impression as you move to a final presentation is to be confident and credible. Do not try too hard to shine. Too much gloss is simply that: gloss. Scratch the surface and there is no depth. We live in an era of spin and marketing hype; our senses are dulled to it. Indeed, many in business react against it.

Echoing one of the key themes of this book, this chapter encourages you to see the world through your buyer's eyes, not your own, and to present your ideas and offerings to the buyer's agenda.

We'll look at five key areas which, if you get them right, reinforce in your buyer's mind that you are different from your competitors:

■ audience

■ structure

■ delivery

■ Q&A

■ visuals.

One other point to make clear is that when we talk about a presentation, it can be one-to-one, to a small group, or to a large group. The setting can be formal or informal, social or business, planned or impromptu, with visuals or without them. We draw the definition very wide and include any occasion where you 'present' your thoughts.

9.1 Audience

Once you've decided what you want to achieve, the next step is to think about your audience.

- What will you do to engage your audience?
- What will you do to demonstrate that you have their best interests at heart?
- How will you address the key areas of money, time and comfort?

Reviewing the responses to questions asked during previous conversations should give you a good idea of what your audience would want to hear about. Use that knowledge to structure your presentation.

Throughout this chapter we will make reference to elements of a communications skills process and workshop called Think on Your Feet® (www.thinkonyourfeet.com). Ideally, you need to take the full two-day workshop, to experience it and then practise. But we can give you a brief idea of how it works.

Think on Your Feet® in brief

Think on Your Feet® is one of those rare things you encounter from time to time – a new way of doing something that can literally change your life. We first encountered Think on Your Feet® in the mid-1990s and have been advocates ever since. We are not easily impressed and have tried dozens of approaches, theories and tools, and read about many more. Many are interesting, but only a rare few are career- and even life-changing.

Think on Your Feet® provides you with real techniques to 'think on your feet' – its major focus. It will also help you put together a presentation.

The elegantly simple approaches within the Think on Your Feet® toolkit work in almost every situation and we have known people use it for everything from chat-up lines, through small and large business gatherings, to weddings and even at a funeral to help keep emotions in check.

The first Think on Your Feet® tool that we look at is the brain-scan grid – a complex name for a very simple tool. The sole aim of this tool is to help you view the world from your buyer's perspective. There are three steps:

1   Consider what you know about your buyer's *background*. Their age,
    family, education, pastimes, personality type (make your best guess),
    attitudes, job role, business goals, personal goals. Also think about
    their background knowledge of both the project and the next
    interaction.
    Then think about their view of you. Do they know you and like you
    (and your organisation)? What are the popular preconceptions about
    your business or profession? How will they expect you to behave? Also
    think about your background knowledge of the project and the
    presentation.

2   Consider what your buyer *hopes* for from the project as a whole and
    from the ideas you will present to them. This is about content and
    style. What are they hoping to hear? What can you say that would be
    to their advantage?

    ▓ In terms of content: ideas; insights; clear messages; competitor
      information; relevant real-life stories; practical application
      examples; costs and benefits; explanation of potential problems
      and solutions.

    ▓ In terms of style: attentiveness (listening); openness; honesty;
      brevity (they are busy people); interest; enthusiasm. Do they want
      detail or big picture? Do they prefer a logical approach or a more
      humanistic approach? Do they want an opportunity to ask
      questions?

3   Finally, think about what will turn them off both in terms of the
    project and your presentation. What might be their *fears* regarding the
    meeting. What would they not want to hear, or not want to happen.

    ▓ In terms of content: complex; too much on product specs and
      technical data; uninteresting; time-consuming; motherhood
      statements and jargon (e.g. world-class, efficient and effective, win-
      win solution); name dropping; unclear or clouded key messages;
      superficial (stories and examples lack depth).

    ▓ In terms of style: pushy; manipulative; arrogant (does not listen);
      superior, formal and distant (talks down to the audience); boring;
      trivial (e.g. too many jokes).

In a grid format, a completed 'brain-scan' looks something like this:

Presenting tours to Hong Kong	To a Japanese Housewives Association	To the England Soccer Supporters Club
Background (What I think about them)	▪ Mostly female ▪ aged 30–50 ▪ polite, even quiet ▪ clean and efficient	▪ Mostly male ▪ aged 20–40 ▪ noisy, fun loving ▪ enjoy drinking
(What they think about me)	▪ No knowledge ▪ expect politeness	▪ No knowledge ▪ suspicious – expect to get ripped-off
Hopes (positives)	▪ Quiet hotel ▪ health spas ▪ close to shopping ▪ good restaurants ▪ bargain prices	▪ Lively area ▪ close to bars ▪ play soccer ▪ lots to do ▪ late morning starts
Fears (negatives)	▪ Cannot understand language ▪ rudeness ▪ too much noise ▪ dirt ▪ being charged inflated prices	▪ Cannot understand language ▪ no soccer ▪ boring nightlife ▪ limited daytime activities

Having completed the grid, each presentation can now be targeted to address the distinct needs of each group. The beauty of this simple tool is that the process becomes second nature. Ultimately you find yourself running through the grid in your mind in a taxi on the way to a meeting, in the lift on the way to the buyer's office and even in the reception while you wait for an appointment. The best thing about the grid is that even if you miss a few points, you will still be much more buyer-focused when you walk into your presentation or meeting.

See how this would work for one of your buyers. Throughout this chapter we will try to help you design a real presentation and plan for dealing with one or two tough questions that you might be asked.

To get started, write in the box below the name(s) of your buyers or the persons you will present to and the subject of your presentation.

Buyer name(s):

Presentation subject:

Now complete the brain-scan grid below for this presentation:

Background
(Them)

(Me)

Hopes (positives)

Fears (negatives)

Let's see how a reappraisal of the audience led to success for Retrams Solicitors.

From my best to what's best for you

Retrams Solicitors was about to make a presentation to the board of BuildMore, a major property company. The solicitors were bidding to win one of their most significant appointments ever, and one which would keep several people employed more or less full-time for up to 10 years.

A proposal had already been submitted. We were asked to help them improve their pitch presentation.

By the time we arrived a team of three presenters had been decided and draft content and running order had been discussed. Retrams were going to use one person to start and close the presentation. The second person would talk about their area of expertise and then the third person would talk about theirs. It was all very logical and would explain very well the capabilities of the firm as they related to this project.

But what about their buyers? What did they want to hear and what would our client do to keep the buyers interested throughout the presentation? What would be different or memorable about it?

We asked a series of questions to understand the buyers' knowledge, hopes and fears. The buyers were a mix of engineers and accountants. They had experience in these kinds of acquisitions, but no experience in the specific assets they had bought. They would be expecting, but may not be wanting, a standard technical presentation on areas of expertise. Since the buyers would already have been meeting all day they may be hard to engage. Retrams were hoping that the buyers would agree, in the meeting, to engage them.

BuildMore had received a technical summary of Retrams's capabilities in advance.

William was the only person from Retrams who knew anyone from BuildMore. Retrams knew little about the individual buyers or their strategy and plans.

The first thing we looked at was what Retrams were trying to achieve. On reflection, Retrams agreed that it was not realistic to expect be engaged as a result of the presentation. A better objective was to get the buyer to agree to a later three-hour workshop where Retrams

▶

could get a better understanding of the buyers' plans and needs, and the buyers could get a better understanding of all the issues.

This fundamentally changed the approach. The key now was to develop a process and content which would persuade the buyers as to the value of spending a further three hours with Retrams. Retrams needed to engage the buyers not impress them.

Retrams had been planning that each of the three present, going through their expertise in a number of areas. Whilst this may have been technically comprehensive, it would not have been enjoyable or memorable – at least not in a positive sense.

It started to look as if the buyers' project had three distinct stages. The application stage, the operations stage and the sales stage. Each of the three Retrams people had expertise that related to each of these three stages. Each of them had stories to tell about occasions where they had saved their clients' time, trouble and money at different phases of similar projects. The sequence of the pitch changed:

Beginning

William – two minutes to introduce and explain the agenda and ask for feedback, additions etc. Also to raise the fact that Retrams feel that at present they do not know enough about the project or the strategy of the buyer to be able to make any meaningful comment on pricing.

Middle

William to set up the presentation on the application stage and to introduce the key points. Shaila, Soraya and William to talk about their experience (rather than expertise) at the application stage of other projects – in that order.

William to summarise and close the application stage, then open the operations stage and introduce the key points. Shaila, Soraya and William to talk about their experience at the operations stage of other projects.

William to close the operations stage and then open the sales stage and introduce the key points. Shaila, Soraya and William to talk about their experience at the sales stage of other projects.

End

William to close the whole presentation and ask for questions. Also to suggest that it occurred to Retrams that there may be value for both parties in having a three-hour workshop within the next couple of weeks to really get into the detail.

The process was now far more engaging. There was also very little explanation of expertise. There was an overall story and within it were a series of shorter stories.

The presentation went ahead, the buyers were engaged throughout and whilst there were some questions at the end they were not very challenging as the team had 'proved' their expertise by recounting stories of their experiences.

The buyers actually suggested, before it was suggested to them, that they needed to get together for a workshop, which they all did.

There are now several Retrams solicitors working very hard to keep up with the project as it goes through the operations stage.

Story-telling

In the example above, the sharing of relevant experience through story-telling was very important. It is puzzling that so few people are comfortable telling stories. Puzzling because everyone has relevant stories to tell. Puzzling because the power of a story to prove capability and to be memorable is very strong.

One explanation often given is that the subject of the story is 'confidential'. But how difficult is it to change the names and other details to make the scenario unrecognisable? True, but then you might get asked about the story, you may say. Possible, but unlikely. And if they do ask, it need not be difficult to answer. If the question targets a sensitive area, it is fine to say, 'I'm sorry but I cannot answer that specific question because it's confidential,' then give a more general response.

Stories, or examples of experience, are important because they are specific and convincing. They give proof.

Consider two examples of a logistics provider talking to a buyer about delivery times:

Without a story	With a story
We have a large air-cargo fleet in the region and we have offices in every major city in China.	Last year one of our customers was in a tight spot. They had late-booked a large conference space only a few days earlier at Taipei's largest computing conference and exhibition, to promote their latest product. They needed to build the conference stand using lighting, service counter equipment and graphic display panels that were scattered in three different locations in China. The conference was only four days away and what had looked like an opportunity was now turning into a crisis.
In Taiwan, we have 150 dedicated staff and the newest fleet of delivery trucks.	
Most of the major technology companies are our clients because they know they can trust us.	
We provide a door-to-door, no-surprises service at competitive rates and we promise that we'll never let you down.	Our people worked double-shifts to collect the goods and bring them to Shanghai. Then we had to route the cargo through Hong Kong to Taipei.
	It arrived in Taipei with two days to spare, but on a public holiday. Staff were called back to work and our entire truck fleet was used to move 150 tons of equipment in four hours.

One example is all motherhood, boasting and promises. The other is proof. It gives comfort that you have been there and dealt with it.

After many years, the authors still do not fully understand why people do not tell more stories. The good news is that if you do, you have a golden opportunity to be both convincing and memorable.

9.2 Structure

A very small percentage of the population are very good at standing in front of a group and presenting their thoughts and ideas. Most of those people work in the entertainment industry; others are politicians. For the rest of us, being confident and credible is as good as it gets. Happily, this is enough. As we mentioned earlier in the book, for many of us, the basis of our confidence in communicating with others is what we know – the content. Unfortunately that can, in itself, cause problems. Fears that you may be wrong, or that someone in the audience may know more than you, can crush the very support mechanism that helps your confidence.

Fortunately, there is another option. Confidence and credibility can be built on structure. Structure is the firm foundation on which any presentation rests.

At the core of Think on Your Feet® are 10 organisational structures (plans) – patterns of communication – which help people achieve three things:

- a focus on what the audience wants to hear, as opposed to what the speaker wants to say
- the ability to give more complete and considered responses to questions
- the presence to stay calm and respond credibly, even when under pressure.

In the following pages we outline some of these simple mental structuring techniques and ask you to apply them to your own situation.

To begin, imagine you are about to make a presentation to a room full of university students. You are going to make a 20-minute presentation on why they should join your organisation. Jot down the outline and key points of your presentation in the box below:

Now, put yourself in the students' shoes and ask yourself these questions:

■ Would you enjoy this presentation; would it grab your interest?

■ Would you believe the presentation addressed your needs or those of the presenter?

■ Would you remember the key messages of the presentation three weeks later?

Look back at section 9.1. Did you do a quick brain-scan grid?
Did it look anything like the one below?

Background (Them)	■ Young, single, starting out in life ■ enthusiastic but sceptical of business and work ■ superficially confident, deep down may be insecure ■ technologically savvy ■ this will be the same as all the other presentations
(Me)	■ Old and out of touch ■ insincere – sure to paint a rosy picture and lure them into working for my company
Hopes (positives)	■ Informative and honest ■ what we would *do* for the first few months and years – talk about learning and development ■ cover work hours, prospects, overseas opportunities, money ■ tell us entry requirements and chances of successful application ■ entertaining – not just a bunch of slides ■ freebies – some giveaways ■ answer our questions ■ short
Fears (negatives)	■ All gloss, no substance – or long and boring ■ full of jargon ■ asks difficult questions (don't want to be embarrassed in front of peers) ■ arrogant and patronising

Completing the grid should help you decide what to include in your presentation. Typically, the challenge for presentations is not about finding sufficient material – you probably jotted down lots of things you could talk to the students about. The challenge lies in organising your ideas into a logical and convincing presentation.

The human brain prefers patterns; it looks for and remembers them. If you can use a pattern that people's brains will hook on to very easily then your chance of communicating effectively will significantly increase.

Keith's wife gives her phone number to people in the following pattern:

122   988   6543

Keith gives people her number in the following pattern:

1229   886   543

Whenever Keith hears her give people her number, he is convinced she has given them the wrong one. Because the pattern is different, his brain short circuits and tells him the number is wrong.

To present successfully, it helps to structure your content in such a way that your recipients' brains can understand and memorise the information. To do this effectively you need to create patterns.

The phone number in the example above followed a 3-3-4 and then a 4-3-3 pattern. How about your own phone number, how do you break it down? Why don't we announce it in, say, 5-2-3 format?

Let's try something. Read the following pairs of letters:

FJ   AF   KH   YT   IG   OR   PE   XQ

Cover up the letters above and write them from memory in the space below.

Now read the following.

KH   PE   KF

Again cover the letters and write the ones you remember below.

There is a very good chance that you remembered all three pairs in the second example, but no more than two pairs in the first example. The reason is that your brain struggles with trying to remember the long sequence and it gets confused.

With this in mind, we advocate keeping the number of key points in any presentation you make to a maximum of four. More than that and your audience will struggle to remember what you were trying to say. Better still, group points in three's – as is stressed in Think on Your Feet®.

Why? There are a number of good reasons, but consider the three most important:

- Three encourages a fuller and more considered response: for example, 'We should eat at the noodle shop tonight' versus 'There are three reasons why we should eat at the noodle shop tonight. First, it is convenient – just down the street, next to the bar, so we can walk to dinner, have something to drink too if we want, and we don't need to worry about who drives home. Second, it's well-priced, not much more than buying the ingredients and cooking it yourself. And third, they're showing the sports match on a big screen!!'

- Two feels adversarial – up or down, in or out, win or lose. Psychologists will often say that you should avoid the either/or scenario because almost by definition there will be a loser. Three feels more comfortable, more objective. Win, lose or draw. Up, down or stay here. In, out or through. With three there is a sense of balance, compromise, wholeness and objectivity.

- Three involves a journey with greater momentum. You want your audience to enjoy the whole communication – you want them to want to hear the next part of what you are going to say. To achieve this you need to take them on a journey. If you only have two points you only have a beginning and an end, and that is not a journey. For a journey you need a middle.

Can you have four points? Yes, if it feels right – but it loses the natural balance and direction that three possesses. Get to five and you're into dangerous territory. Reach six and. . .split into two groups of three!

Now, with this 'rule of three' in mind, one final thought. It is also important to connect the three points. If you can then after your presentation your listener only needs to remember one of the points, because the others are connected so they should find them relatively easy to recall, once they have one of the three. If you have three disparate points then your listener will find it hard to remember them all.

Look back to the recruitment presentation you scripted earlier in this chapter. Write in the box below the three points that you think the graduates are most interested in listening to.

```
1


2


3
```

Similarly, for the real presentation for which you did the brain-scan grid earlier, list the three key points you want to get across.

```
1


2


3
```

Now you have a structure that will help make sure you address the key points your buyer cares about. This means it is more likely that you will keep their interest whilst you are talking.

The full Think on Your Feet® approach includes three informative structures (or plans), three persuasive structures and four supportive structures. We cover only the three informative plans here. For details on the other structures, and the workshop itself, visit www.thinkonyourfeet.com.

The plans can be used in any situation, but some are particularly useful in certain situations and for specific types of people.

The Clock Plan

Tell your story from three points (or 'pegs') in time, for example:

- morning, noon and night
- short term, medium term and long term
- junior school, high school and university.

Clock plans are particularly useful for dealing with situations where you have been accused of something. Using the clock plan to frame your response will stop you being defensive and set your audience on the path to resolution.

'I am really sorry that the shop display was not completed to your satisfaction.

- This afternoon I will pull the team together to discuss how we can put things right,
- by lunchtime tomorrow we will deliver a revised design to you, and
- by the end of Wednesday I will organise a work team to implement the new design.'

The clock plan is particularly effective to use with a buyer who likes structure and is an organised thinker.

Now for the recruitment presentation. List down the three pegs in time that you think the graduates are most interested in listening to. Note that these pegs may not match the key points for the presentation that you noted down earlier.

```
1


2


3
```

For your real presentation, do the same: list three pegs in time that may work as hooks for the content you want to communicate.

```
1


2


3
```

The Globe Plan

Tell your story by reference to three locations, for example:

■ France, China and the US

■ Home, office and the bar

■ Top, middle and bottom.

Particularly useful for big issues as it tends to be pictorial and people can 'see' the places you talk about.

'Looking at our plans for next year, let me tell you about how:

■ *At customer sites, we plan to spend more time with buyers and users*

■ *in our offices, we intend to install new systems to facilitate greater sharing of knowledge, and*

■ *at home, we want our people to relax, so we're encouraging employees to cut connections to the workplace once they get home – phones off, Blackberries off.'*

The globe plan is very good for people who like to draw comparisons in order to see the 'big picture'. In Europe they do it this way; in Asia they do it another way; in the US they do it any way they like!

Going back to the recruitment presentation, list down three places that you think the graduates are most interested in hearing about. These may or may not be any of the same key points you listed above.

1

2

3

For your real presentation list three locations that work as pegs for your information.

```
1


2


3
```

The Perspectives Plan

Tell your story from three different people's viewpoints, for example:

■ clients, staff and the board

■ wife, son and mother-in-law

■ economic buyer, user buyer and technical buyer.

This plan is particularly useful for taking the tension out of a situation where there is a potential conflict or difference of opinion, since it encourages the audience to look at things differently. It also makes the speaker appear thoughtful and objective – capable of looking at issues from many angles in a calm and dispassionate manner.

'Lets look at your pay rise request from:

■ *your perspective*

■ *the perspective of the other members of the team, and*

■ *from the perspective of the management group.'*

The perspectives plan is very good for people who prefer the emotional and humanistic side of things.

For the recruitment presentation list how joining your organisation looks to three different people or bodies of people.

1 From the perspective of

2 From the perspective of

3 From the perspective of

For your real presentation list how three different people or bodies of people might look at your content.

1 From the perspective of

2 From the perspective of

3 From the perspective of

It is likely that you found one of these plans easier to develop than the others. This could be for one of three reasons:

- The subject matter lends itself better to one plan than the other.
- You felt the buyer would prefer one over the other.
- You have a natural preference for one over the other.

If it is the latter, then you can also use the plans as a way to challenge your preferred thinking and perhaps come up with a structure and a story that is more tuned into your buyer's needs and preferences, rather than your own.

9.3 Delivery

Imagine you sell water. You are about to pitch the sale of a new brand of flavoured water to the CEO of a major supermarket chain. Write down, in full, what you would say, using one of the three plans. Make sure you write the actual words you would use.

Plan (circle your choice):   **Clock**   **Globe**   **Perspectives**

1

2

3

When you've done this, turn the page.

Now, count the occurrences of the following words:

| *we; my; our; it; [our company name]* | *Number of occurrences:* | |

Then count the occurrences of the words:

| *you; your; [their company name]* | *Number of occurrences:* | |

Focusing on the value to the buyer

If your words are primarily in the first group then your plan is focused on the features of the flavoured water. This is what most salespeople do – talk about the features of their offering. Unfortunately, what they are not doing is talking about the benefit or value to the buyer. The difference from the buyer's perspective is enormous.

If you go into a clothes shop and the shop assistant says one of the following two things:

- This is a really good shirt.
- You look really good in that shirt.

Which is the more powerful?

Applying this to the previous example of flavoured water, you might have said the following:

Clock

1. Ten years ago, you sold 2,000 litres of bottled water each week, with just a few brands available and consistent margins.
2. Today, your weekly sales are in the region of 20,000 litres each week with maybe a dozen brands available with varying margins.
3. Looking forward one year, with this new line of flavoured water, you should be aiming at sales of 30,000 litres each week, and at higher margins.

Globe

The majority of your sales come from three locations:

1. Your convenience outlet in the petrol station sells 2,000 litres of bottled water each week
2. Your small supermarket in the town centre sells 3,000 litres each week
3. Your megastore on the edge of town sells 15,000 litres each week.

Perspectives

Flavoured water increases sales because it opens up new markets for you – specifically younger people and schoolchildren. Support for these sugar-free drinks has come from three key groups:

1. The medical profession who tell us that sugar-related diabetic illness is out of control and more sugar-free food and drinks are a must
2. Parents concerned about the health of their children
3. Children themselves, who tell us that these flavoured waters are more refreshing than other drinks and don't leave them craving more liquids.

If you really struggled to come up with three values or benefits then we would argue that this flavoured water is not for that buyer. An I Owe U salesperson would quickly recognise if this were the case, and would move on, not wanting to waste either their own or the buyer's time.

To make your ideas even more convincing, try explicitly to link the features of your offering to the value or benefit to the listener. Too many people state the features of their offering and expect the buyer to join the dots and understand the value or benefit. After all, the value is obvious – right?

Well it is to you (since you know your offering so well), but perhaps not to the buyer. Even if it is obvious to the buyer, it may not be obvious to their colleagues, who may have an influence on the buying decision.

Failing to explicitly state the value or benefit attaching to a feature of your offering gives an opportunity to your competitor to establish in your buyers' minds that they are more focused than you are on the benefit that they, the buyers, will derive.

Taking the example of the logistics provider mentioned earlier in this chapter:

Feature	Benefit
1. We have the largest air cargo fleet in the region.	Which means that if you face an urgent deadline we can move large shipments very fast, saving you time and worry.
2. We have offices in all the major Chinese cities.	So if items from disparate locations need to be shipped together, we can easily collect them and send a consolidated shipment, saving time, cost and trouble at the destination matching items from different consignments.
3. At the destination we maintain a new fleet of road vehicles.	Because we know there is nothing more frustrating than having goods at the point of destination that cannot be delivered to customers because vehicles are not available or have broken down. Our fleet enables us to give a 100% delivery guarantee which lets you sleep at night without worries.

Focusing on the value or benefit to the buyer demonstrates appreciation of their situation and is more persuasive. Arguably the reason people stop after only stating features is because that is the easy part. Linking to benefits is harder.

Fortunately though, it is not much harder, you just need to develop the habit of continually challenging yourself by asking 'So what?' For example:

We are the biggest selling sportswear manufacturer in the world	So what?
We have more product choice than other manufacturers	So what?
Well, in Asia for example it means that we have the scale to set up a specialist design centre to design clothes to suit the Asian body-shape rather than the US or European body shape	So what?
You get clothes that fit you properly	So what?
It makes you look good, feel good and perform better at the sports you play	OK!

So the sales pitch changes from:

'You should buy from us because we are the biggest'

to

'You will have sportswear that looks better, feels better and ultimately enhances your sense of well-being and your athletic performance. To achieve this, we use our scale and buying power to source materials and design products that are tailored to the body-shape of each market.'

Wow – I'll have some of that!

Now, take the same thinking and apply it to your real presentation, jotting down your possible words in the table overleaf. Before you do this though, you do need to think about your real buyer and decide what the value points are to them.

Once you have done this you need to decide which of the three plans is most effective.

There could be a temptation to use the one you are most comfortable with, or the one which best describes what it is you are trying to sell, but remember – it's about the buyer's needs.

You need to consider the way your buyer prefers to think. If they like structure, then a clock works; if they like the big picture then the globe; if they are concerned about people then the perspectives plan.

Follow these guidelines and your buyers will find your presentation more enjoyable and memorable. You might enjoy it more too.

Doing the best that you can

We said earlier that structure underpins a good, buyer-focused presentation, helping you make an impression as a credible, confident person – someone who inspires confidence and trust.

There are other things to think about when you find yourself asked to present your ideas and we list these here for you to consider as a checklist when planning for a one-to-one meeting or a presentation to a larger group:

Matching

■ If there is to be a panel, think about who goes. Match your people to buyers. Sit them opposite the buyers whose personalities they match

Clock

1

2

3

Globe

1

2

3

Perspectives

1

2

3

the closest and think about what they can say to reinforce any personal chemistry.

■ Try not to go alone. If you are on your own, even in a one-to-one situation, it inhibits your ability to step out of the content and consider the behavioural and interpersonal aspects.

Body language and gestures

■ Think about body language, especially use of hand gestures. Do they help reinforce or do they distract?

■ Remember to nod, either when the buyer makes a particularly strong point (don't do it all the time or you'll look silly!) or when one of your colleagues makes a point.

■ Walking around. Some people say don't do it but generally we don't agree. If walking around makes you feel more comfortable and relaxed, do it. But don't overdo it!

The location

■ The rule of thumb with meeting and presentation locations is to make them comfortable for you. Try not to allow the venue to dictate the way that you present.

■ Think about the location, check the address and arrive early to set up and settle down. David confesses to once turning up at the wrong building to present to a panel of five people who were in the company's other main building. He finally arrived 15 minutes late, obviously flustered and had to go straight into his presentation. No time to settle down. He didn't get the job.

■ If you are offered microphones, think carefully before accepting. Using a microphone sometimes means that the speaker changes their natural behaviour and style to accommodate the microphone, consequently they often do not appear as natural and confident. This is especially true of hand-held microphones. If you must use a microphone always try to get a clip one.

■ If the seating is pre-arranged in a way that you do not think helps you, check whether you can change it.

Engaging your audience

■ For ideas about what to do in a one-to-one situation, see Chapter 5. For larger audiences, consider asking about your audience's experience

– something you need to know so that you can customise the content of your presentation (e.g. How long have you worked in the company or industry?). The key is to ask a question that is easy for your audience to answer, is linked to your topic and provides you with some information as well as steadying any nerves that you might have.

9.4 Pulling it all together

If you are making a longer presentation then having three points is not enough to hold the content together in an effective way. In these cases you need to develop layers of plans.

For example, if you were making a long presentation to graduates on why they should join your company you could use the following structure.

Main plan	Main plan points	Secondary plan and points
Clock	1 First part of your career	**Globe** 1 Work at the office 2 Work at the client site 3 Work from home
	2 After three years	**Perspectives** 1 Your bosses 2 Your peers 3 Your subordinates
	3 After six years	**Benefits** 1 Financial 2 Status 3 Challenge

One other beauty of this approach – you can design presentations very quickly.

Test this out. Write down the three key points you would use to sell to your buyer the value of your offering using the three different plans:

Main plan	Main plan points	Secondary plan and points
Clock		
	1	
		1
		2
		3
	2	
		1
		2
		3
	3	
		1
		2
		3
Globe		
	1	
		1
		2
		3
	2	
		1
		2
		3
	3	
		1
		2
		3
Perspectives		
	1	
		1
		2
		3
	2	
		1
		2
		3
	3	
		1
		2

9.5 Q&A

In a pitch situation, sensible people will rehearse their presentations. The *most* sensible people will also prepare for the Q&A that comes at the end.

Increasingly, because the sensible people are rehearsing their presentations, buyers are finding it more difficult to justify eliminating bidders based on their presentations and are placing more reliance on the destructive capability of the Q&A session. If this sounds negative, remember what we said at the very start of this chapter. The good I Owe U salesperson will normally have already won the hearts and minds of the buyer long before the pitch meeting or 'beauty parade' (as they are sometimes called).

Of course, there are situations where there are two bidders who are difficult to separate and so presentations are requested. In such situations, the presentations are typically an echo of what has been said previously – it is the Q&A that invariably decides the outcome.

A few years ago, David was asked to advise a major auditing firm in connection with one of their important clients, worth over US$2 million in annual fees, that had put their audit services out to tender. David's client, Firm A, were the incumbents. In true I Owe U fashion, David advised Firm A that they should seek meetings with all the key players and find out their ambitions, challenges and expectations of how Firm A might help.

The response was shocking to the proposal team. They met a wave of criticism of the service they had received in recent years. That was part of the reason for going out to tender. The team was devastated. How could they win?

There was only one way. Admit past errors and focus on how service would be different going forward. Not just promises, but step-by-step plans for achieving and measuring the projected improvements. This was laid out in the proposal document and Firm A was asked to present. Two days before the final meeting, the client said there would be Q&A only.

Fortunately, David and the team had rehearsed three Q&A sessions, imagining the most searching questions that the client might ask. The answers had been evaluated and tightened, to give greater clarity and impact. The meeting day came, the questions asked were tough, but 90% of them had been covered in the rehearsals. Firm A retained the client.

As often happens, Firm A was able to find out, through friendly channels, how the decision was made. Firm D had fallen at the first hurdle – their proposal document failing to impress. Firm C had performed poorly in the Q&A. Firm B, the main competitor to Firm A had, as expected, fielded a strong team and offered a significantly lower fee. However, in the Q&A, while they answered confidently, their answers were described as 'a bit generic'. Firm A's responses on the other hand were crisp and comprehensive.

The job was won in the Q&A session.

For some people, being asked a question in a presentation situation is the worst thing that can happen. It can mean:

■ You may have said something that is wrong.

■ You may not have covered everything.

■ Someone in your audience may know more than you do and is determined to show it.

Worse still:

■ Someone may ask you a question to which you *do not know the answer.*

■ Someone may ask you a question which *you do not want to answer.*

■ Someone may *challenge what you have said.*

In each of these situations, it is likely that the presenter will have problems gathering their thoughts and giving a reasoned answer. How often have you seen someone get asked a question and respond immediately, talking away but not making much sense? You can almost sense the wheels turning in their mind as they search for ideas and finally, many words after they started to answer, they begin to talk sense.

Unfortunately, what has happened in such situations is a physiological reaction, designed for a time when we ran from dinosaurs and animals with large claws and teeth. When we feel threatened – and to be asked an uncomfortable question triggers a sense that we are being attacked – our bodies release chemicals that tell our brains to release oxygen to our main muscle groups in order that they can perform at optimum capacity while we fight or run away. That oxygen is released from the organ that uses the most oxygen: the brain.

So, in the modern business world, where threats often come in the form of unanticipated tough questions, our brains can let us down right at the point we need them most.

What we need is a way to stop ourselves giving an incoherent, rambling response while our body calms down and releases oxygen back to the brain. Think on Your Feet®, the approach we mentioned earlier, also outlines three ways to deal with unexpected and tough questions. These are collectively referred to as 'bridging techniques', enabling a person to bridge gracefully from tough question to structured answer. The three options include:

■ **acknowledge** (e.g. That's a good question; I've been asked similar questions before; I can see how that might be a concern)

■ **adapt** (e.g. So what you're really saying is . . .; if I understand you correctly, what you're asking is. . .)

■ **ask** (e.g. What element of X is it that you think led to the problem? Is there a particular aspect of Y that concerns you? What do you see as the impact of X? Before I respond, can you just tell me what is it about X that is so important to you?).

A fourth option is to ask the other person to repeat the question, but this can be used only once. It is necessary though when you have been asked a multi-part question and that is quite common.

To see how this works, consider our flavoured water salesperson. The supermarket CEO, unconvinced by the vision of huge sales of flavoured water, says:

'Surely this is just another fad, like the high-performance sports water you launched last year that failed to achieve its targets and left me with a warehouse full of unsold product.'

Acknowledge	'I can see that a warehouse full of unsold water would not be something you would want to happen again. Let me tell you why the flavoured water will be a success and how we can make sure you are not left with large unsold stock.'
Adapt	'That's a very good point and setting realistic sales targets is important. Let me explain how we set the sales targets this time around.'
Ask	'Before I answer that, I'd be interested to hear your thoughts on why the performance water was less successful than we had all thought it would be?'

Now, think about the presentation that you have been working on throughout this chapter. What would be a question you would not want to be asked?

Your difficult question:

Now write down your bridge from question to answer:

Acknowledge

Adapt

Ask

Now think about how to give a convincing answer using the three Think on Your Feet® plans we introduced earlier:

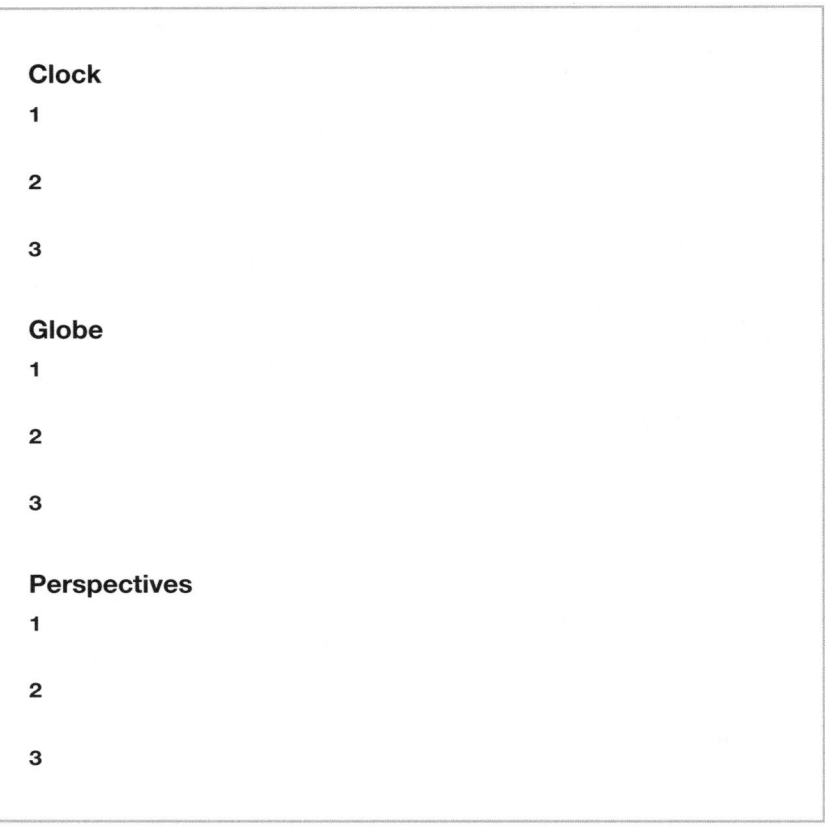

Clock

1

2

3

Globe

1

2

3

Perspectives

1

2

3

Repeat this exercise for the questions you sometimes get asked that you really do not like. As a result, you will respond more confidently and credibly the next time you are asked.

9.6 Visuals

One thought regarding presentations. If you need a support mechanism, such as notes or a slide deck, to remind you what you are going to say, how can you expect your audience to remember it in the future?

Twenty years ago visuals were called visual aids. If someone wheeled out a projector or had put together some computer-based slides (as we used to call them), there was a certain novelty value. It made an impact. That has

all changed. How many presentations have you attended where the presenter used a technology medium as a key part of the presentation. Almost
all of them?

And that is one of the problems. We have all been subjected to so much
'death by slides' that visuals, at least slide visuals, tend to wash over us. The
whole point of visual aids is to act as an aid – rarely the case these days.

The problem of course is that many slide visuals are not visuals at all. They
are text messages placed on a background (resplendent with a corporate
logo) and projected onto a screen, possibly accompanied by a clip-art image
or photograph that bears some relation to the words on the slide. Often
there are too many words, often the presenter simply reads off the slides.
None of which makes a good impression.

Another challenge with slides is that too many people tell themselves that
they are ready for a presentation based on the fact that they've written their
slides. That does not mean they are ready for their presentation – it just
means they have written their slides.

So, our advice would be to sketch out your presentation outline and decide
your key messages before going anywhere near designing your slides. And
if you can get your message across without using slides, so much the better.
You'll be different and the audience will remember more of your message.

If you must use slides, and sometimes they can be useful, particularly for
longer presentations, multiple languages and larger audiences, remember
the following:

▦ Visuals should be helpful to the audience, echoing the presentation
  structure and reinforcing key points.

▦ End each slide with a summary of that slide's key message (which
  should be clear from the slide).

▦ Visuals should be consistent and attractive, without distracting effects
  such as multiple screen transitions.

▦ Leave sufficient time for the audience to read. How irritating is it
  when someone quickly shows a slide and then says, 'That wasn't
  important, let's move on'?

▦ Even more irritating, show someone a screen filled with numbers that
  they cannot read and say, 'I know you cannot read this but. . .'

▦ Avoid reading your slide with your back to your audience.

▦ Avoid laser pointers – they can be distracting and irritating.

- Avoid remote pointers – or at least make sure you know which keyboard keys to use to move forwards and backwards – just in case the remote fails.
- Use the 'B' key when showing the presentation to toggle 'Black' on and off. Very useful.

In short, handle with care. Slides are the most overused and ineffective (if not negative) presentation medium available.

Following the tips and structures detailed in this chapter will ensure that any time you are called upon to outline your ideas you will be able to perform with confidence and credibility – potentially career defining moments.

In the next chapter we bring together all the elements of the I Owe U approach and provide a few final thoughts on how to put I Owe U to work.

Hotel Ltd – part 2

This time Richard and Emily decided to differentiate themselves by the way they presented.

They determined the three key points that were important to Hotel. They also decided the most effective way to tell their story was by looking at what their offering would mean to the staff at Hotel, the buyers that they were addressing and the shareholders.

They focused on the benefits to those three groups. They did not use slides.

There were no interruptions and they handled one really hard question – *how would they implement the offering* – talking through the scoping, design and implementation phases, and giving one example each of the problems encountered on similar implementations, how they had been addressed and the lessons learned.

The conversation then moved into a discussion of when they could start the scoping phase.

Key messages

- Put yourself in the shoes of the buyer.
- Tell a story.
- Acknowledge the importance of patterns.
- Remember and apply the rule of three.
- Focus on the benefit or value to the buyer.
- Visuals should only be used if they add value to the audience.

10

Getting smarter – putting I Owe U to work

'To give real service you must add something which cannot be bought or measured with money, and that is sincerity and integrity.'

Douglas Adams, Author (1952–2001)

In this chapter we look back at everything we have covered in the book, and forward to what you need to do to implement the skills and tools – aligned with your growing awareness of how to differentiate your ideas, services or products – and yourself.

Offering yourself

Richard and Emily have a new offering – themselves. They have decided that buyers purchase their product more often and pay more if they focus on adding value to the buyer all the way through the process.

They also know that Emily is a big picture person who likes to thrash ideas around whilst Richard is the perfectionist who prefers his own company to big groups.

The planning form they now use for meetings looks like this.

▶

Buyer company name		Buyer individual name	
Industry		Personality of buyer	
Economic, user or technical buyer		Contact history	
What was said in the last meeting?		Where is meeting to be held?	
Relationship	Now	In 1 month	In 3 months
Buyer's issues	Current state	Desired state	Value in shift

They find this helps them focus on the right things before and during meetings.

They've identified TBend Inc. (a rubber product manufacturer) as a potential buyer of their hardware, software and ongoing service.

They've web researched all they can about the company and the names of the IT and HR directors and the CFO. It turns out that Paul, a friend of Emily's, knows the HR Director, Simon Stoke, very well. Emily spends some time with Paul finding out about Simon – his role, the things he likes and also some rumours about the challenges he faces at TBend.

Paul mentioned Emily's name to Simon and he seemed happy to hear from her.

Emily and Richard spent an hour together discussing their strategy before meeting Simon. During this meeting they considered the type

▶

of person Simon might be and they wrote the IOU that Emily would use to make a phonecall to him. They agreed the aim of the call was to arrange a one-hour meeting between Emily, Richard and Simon.

Emily then called Simon and used IOU to ask whether Simon would be interested in meeting so that each party could learn more about the other. They talked for 15 minutes and Simon agreed to see Emily and Richard the next week for an hour.

Emily and Richard reconvened to talk about the things Simon had said and how he came across. It appeared that Simon was a fairly quiet individual who tended not to lead discussions and was a very organised thinker. They decided they would run the meeting by finding out what challenges Simon was facing, even though none of them may be IT-related.

They also word processed a very brief summary of the conversation that Emily had with Simon and sent it to Simon via email together with confirmation of the location, timing and objectives of next meeting.

Emily and Richard then did their final planning for the meeting. They agreed that Emily would do the IOU but that Richard would do most of the questioning as he seemed closer in personality to Simon. Emily would also do most of the writing.

Following the introductions, Emily started the meeting by saying, 'Thank you for taking the time to speak to me and Richard. What we would like to do is get a good understanding of the main issues and opportunities that you face. The way we would like to do this is through asking some questions and listening to what is on your mind. Clearly, in the future, we would like to be able to help you, however in this meeting we will not be trying to sell you anything – just finding out what needs you may have. By the end of the meeting we hope that some of the experiences that we share will be of use to you.'

At the meeting Emily asked permission to take notes. Once Simon had agreed she introduced the Value-Sheet approach and said she would give Simon a copy at the end of the meeting.

They completed the following Value-Sheet document.

Issue	Current	Desired	Value
Staff attrition rates	38% across the business, 42% for females and 34% for males. This is costing a lot in recruitment and retraining and there is also a question on how much this is affecting quality and the business's culture.	25% across the business within three years.	$2 million in recruitment and retraining costs, but also significant saving in the time Simon spends dealing with recruitment and exits.
Access to and impact on leadership strategy	They have a lot of key performance indicators in various divisions and at different levels, but they appear inconsistent and it is proving hard to get buy-in as many people don't see how they fit with business strategy.	To be on the leadership team and in a position to influence KPI's and their communication to all employees.	
360-degree feedback process	The feedback process is half automated and half manual. It takes a lot of time and resources and there have been errors as well.	A totally automated system that everyone trusts and uses properly.	Will save time and provide speedier and more comprehensive guidance to management.

At the end of the meeting Emily recapped on the key points and closed the meeting by suggesting that she calls Simon in a few days to progress any ideas.

When they got back to the office Emily typed the table above and sent it, with a CC letter via email, saying that she would call Simon on Tuesday afternoon to check that she had covered all the points that they had discussed.

Richard and Emily are an invented pair of salespeople. However their story is partly a reflection of the journey that we, the authors, have taken and partly a collection of real stories we have seen up close in our careers.

You may still be thinking that whatever good ideas we have put forward in this book they are not really appropriate or effective in a salesperson's world. Therein lies the problem. It is not a salesperson's world, it is a buyer's world.

Below are three major reasons why we believe our ideas will make you more effective at selling.

- Business has changed. It has become more empathetic and community driven. Doing the right thing is now seen as important.

  Take a look at the request for proposal documents coming from large corporations. No matter what business they or you are in there will be a section requiring you to comply with their corporate responsibility and sustainability regulations.

- Whatever it is you are trying to sell there is more competition than ever before. People have easy access to products from around the world and businesses are diversifying into new industries and new markets.

  You are having to compete with a much greater number of other people and organisations offering something very similar. If you don't get the relationship right your only differentiator is price – a very dangerous place to be.

- Generation Y are driven by much more than money: they are driven by challenge, growth and relationships.

  Whilst this generation may be much younger than you, they are now moving up to middle management. They are becoming the economic buyers. If they cannot relate to you then they are unlikely to buy from you.

With all this in mind you need to develop a mindset of wanting to *help* your buyer rather than trying to sell to your buyer.

Once you have developed that mindset, we believe that if you remember the key points below you will not only 'truly' help your buyer, you will become significantly more successful as a salesperson and will find your career more rewarding.

1 Yourself

- Recognise your natural behaviour.
- Learn to understand and control yourself.
- Really listen and don't just wait for your turn to speak.
- Don't disappear once you have made the sale.
- Don't move into action too soon.
- Develop a mindset which says 'No' to proposals.

2 Your buyer

- Each buyer has a different personality, buying style and need.
- Give the buyer control of the conversation.
- Don't assume anything about your buyer.
- Be there even when the buyer does not need your offering, but could value your input.
- Reward the buyer for the time and money they are investing in you.
- Match the buyer's behaviour to build rapport.
- Understand the relationship you have with your buyer – from their perspective.
- Aim for a partner relationship.
- Focus on the benefits to the buyer of your offering.

3 Processes

- Use I Owe U to start meetings and give your buyer control.
- Use SHAPE to uncover the real needs of the buyer.
- Use Value-Sheets to help meetings through identifying needs, desired positions and value for the buyer.
- Try to move from level 1 to level 4 to deal with the real issue.
- Use the CC letter to continue the collaborative process.
- Provide proof of capability through storytelling.
- Use the rule of three when presenting ideas or answers.

Above all, remember that buying is an emotional decision. As Ford Harding (*Rain Making*, 1994) reminds us:

'People buy on feelings and use facts to justify what they feel.'

And the journey continues

We are here to help you on your journey. For more guidance, or to access copies of the tools included in the book, please contact us at keith.dugdale@ioweu.com or david.lambert@ioweu.com or sign into the web site www.ioweu.com.

We will do whatever we can to help you.

We Owe U.

11

Summary of key messages

Chapter 1 I Owe U – next generation sales strategies

- Too many buyer–seller relationships are deficient in trust, enjoyment and shared commitment.
- 'Push' sales methods are increasingly counter-productive since every buyer and every conversation is unique. Prescriptive approaches will not work.
- Consultative sales approaches focus more on buyers' needs, but can also be manipulative – targeting areas of interest to sellers rather than buyers.
- I Owe U is a next-generation consultative approach that takes the buyer on a more natural and engaging sales journey – differentiating the seller from the competition.
- In conversations, control rests with the buyer, with the salesperson following the buyer's thoughts.
- The salesperson must recognise that they have a responsibility to the buyer that goes beyond securing the current sale.

Chapter 2 How other people really see you

- Self understanding – of your behavioural preferences, and how these affect others, is the starting point for building better relationships.
- You cannot decide to change your personality, but you can decide to change your outward behaviour – if you so choose.
- The way that you behave determines the way that others behave towards you.

■ Behaviours must be genuine. False behaviours are quickly seen for what they are.

■ There is a strong positive correlation between high Octagon™ scores and I Owe U sales success – especially in trust, your needs and feelings.

Chapter 3   Understanding and changing your relationships

■ In order to change a relationship, you first need to understand what relationship you have.

■ Seller–buyer relationships may be classified as ad-hoc, technical, social or partner.

■ There are advantages and disadvantages associated with each type of relationship. I Owe U salespeople aim for 'partner' relationships.

■ Many salespeople overestimate the strength of their relationships with their buyers.

■ Moving a relationship is often a matter of adopting a helping mindset and the right strategies – stopping to think before each interaction with the buyer and planning a consistent approach over time.

■ Sometimes it is easier to introduce a new person in order to change a relationship than it is to break the current pattern.

Chapter 4 Understanding and adapting to buyers

■ Every buyer is different – do not rely on stereotypes.

■ Understand buyer types – economic, user and technical – and the criteria they will use for buying and the influence they will have on the buying decision.

■ Understand buyer roles – sponsor, anti-sponsor, coach and gatekeeper – and how best to manage them in your buying process.

■ Think carefully about buyers' personalities and how you can adjust your behaviour to match theirs.

■ Periodically ask buyers for feedback on their perceptions of their relationships with you and your organisation.

Chapter 5 Building rapport and trust – the I Owe U approach

- Buyers expect that you will push them to buy.

- Differentiate yourself from your competitors by displaying a strong desire to understand issues and share experience.

- Use the I Owe U approach to start a collaborative journey by explicitly offering control of conversations to the buyer.

- Reward buyers for the time they are investing.

Chapter 6 Uncovering real needs

- Avoid assumptions.

- Stay in step with the buyer, responding to their moves – as opposed to taking control and forcing the pace.

- SHAPE the process to ensure you arrive at a solid, shared understanding of prioritised needs.

  Surface – to elicit facts.

  Hunt   – to understand the challenges/problems behind the facts.

  Adjust – to ask permission, confirm priority or change direction.

  Paint – the outcomes/benefits of taking action.

  Engage – agree next steps.

- Ease your way into SHAPE by memorising key drivers of concern and adding variety through the use of 'spicy' questions.

- Use Value-Sheets to display structure, understanding and a desire to deliver value.

- Always retain a 'helping' mindset to assist the buyer in articulating their needs.

Chapter 7 Moving to a higher level

- Understand the value of moving conversations to the 'big picture'.

- Recognise that thinking occurs at different levels.

- Understand your own natural thinking level and flex this to match your buyer's preferred level.

- Move from level 1 to level 4 by using unblocking Paint questions or Spicy Questions.

- Don't move to action points too soon in the process.

Chapter 8　Cementing credibility and trust

- Use CC letters to confirm shared understanding and continue the collaborative process.
- Develop a mindset that avoids written proposals unless absolutely necessary.
- Provide proof of capability through sharing experience – both the good and the bad.

Chapter 9　Presenting ideas for positive impact

- Put yourself in the buyer's shoes.
- Tell a story.
- The importance of patterns.
- Remember and apply the rule of three.
- Focus on the benefit or value to the buyer.
- Visuals should only be used if they add value for the audience.

Appendix 1: Your Octagon™ behavioural assessment

Complete your assessment by placing a tick in one box for each statement that most closely describes you. Answer quickly, instinctively and honestly.

Category 1	Always	Most of the time	On occasion	Never
I prefer to make decisions rather than follow someone else's lead				
I prefer to follow someone else rather than take the lead				
In a meeting I tend to keep quiet even when I disagree rather than speak out				
I will make suggestions rather than wait for others to do so				
I prefer to see what others have to say before I say anything				
I will defer to leadership rather than challenge it				
I leave decisions to others rather than make them myself				
People tend to expect me to take control				
I tend to say what I think				

Category 2	Always	Most of the time	On occasion	Never
My friends/colleagues view me as a cautious person				
I regard myself as practical				
I tend to look at the risks rather than at the possibilities				
I would rather look at reality than an imagined future				
It is more important to be correct than adventurous in thinking				
Planning in detail is more effective than rushing to a decision				
Before going into a big meeting I like to cover all the bases				
I like sticking to the rules				
Failure is not trying rather than not succeeding				

Category 3	Always	Most of the time	On occasion	Never
I find it easier to relate to people than to technology				
I tend to prefer group decisions over individual leadership				
Making up my own mind is generally more effective than consulting with the team				
People should behave in accordance with corporate objectives, rather than determine their own goals				
Rules of operation are more important than freedom of choice				
Teams need rules as they will tend to become inefficient if given too much freedom				
I tend to ask closed and leading questions in order to speed up the process				
I am happy working on my own and don't need others				
If I let my guard down people may take advantage of me				

Category 4	Always	Most of the time	On occasion	Never
My friends/colleagues would say I do things with other peoples' interests at heart				
Sometimes I find it hard to find a balance between my personal needs and those of my team				
I assume everyone else is most interested in looking after their own needs				
I am motivated to understand my buyers' needs rather than sell them my ideas				
I listen to the views of my team members rather than impart my own				
I can trust my team to make decisions about new and complex problems				
When I challenge someone's thinking it is always in order to help them, rather than to promote my opinion				
I start conversations with a question rather than a statement				
I challenge people with what I know				

Category 5	Always	Most of the time	On occasion	Never
When making decisions I tend to react with 'gut' feeling				
I like to know what my colleagues are thinking				
My friends/colleagues view me as a highly rational person				
I prefer to deal with someone in person rather than in writing				
I am more comfortable with facts than feelings				
If I get a 'gut' feeling about a business decision, or an intuitive reaction to a person, I do not ignore it				
My friends/colleagues view me as a compassionate person				
My colleagues would see me as open and caring				
I worry about how my team is feeling				

Category 6	Always	Most of the time	On occasion	Never
I like to get one thing done before moving to another				
I like to have a to-do list				
My staff view me as easy going				
I do not mind being unprepared for meetings				
I prefer to have regular rather than impromptu meetings				
When going on holiday, I tend to have detailed travel plans				
My personal preference is not to have an open-door policy to staff, but to have regular meetings				
I prefer not to have an agenda for meetings				
I am an organised thinker				

Category 7	Always	Most of the time	On occasion	Never
If something is not broken I tend to leave it as it is				
I tend to judge my performance against that of other people				
I like to be sure we will win assignments and just doing our best is not enough				
I am motivated to better myself more than to worry about how others are performing				
I am motivated to be the highest performer in my team				
I tend to ask people to justify ideas first before agreeing with them				
I am more interested in what someone can do for me than I am in what I can do for them				
I am an optimistic person				
Knowing what my competition is doing is more important than just focusing on my own performance				

Category 8	Always	Most of the time	On occasion	Never
I like to work at doing the same thing better before moving on to doing different things				
I think the best ideas come from thinking about them				
Leadership should be done by the most senior person				
I tend to get other people to attend to the detail of decisions while I deal with the big picture				
Dreams are great but reality is more important				
I like to make sure things are perfect rather than just OK				
People seek me out for what I know more than how I interact				
People say I have lots of ideas, but they see many of them as unrealistic				
I tend to have ideas without any obvious rationale				

Scoring your answers

The next stage is to understand what your answers mean in terms of your behaviour. Circle the number that relates to the answer you selected and then add up the total of the numbers you have circled.

Category 1	Always	Most of the time	On occasion	Never
I prefer to make decisions rather than follow someone else's lead	20	15	5	0
I prefer to follow someone else rather than take the lead	0	5	15	20
In a meeting I tend to keep quiet even when I disagree rather than speak out	0	5	15	20
I will make suggestions rather than wait for others to do so	20	15	5	0
I prefer to see what others have to say before I say anything	0	5	15	20
I will defer to leadership rather than challenge it	0	5	15	20
I leave decisions to others rather than make them myself	0	5	15	20
People tend to expect me to take control	20	15	5	0
I tend to say what I think	20	15	5	0
Total for Leading / Following				

Category 2	Always	Most of the time	On occasion	Never
My friends/colleagues view me as a cautious person	0	5	15	20
I regard myself as practical	0	5	15	20
I tend to look at the risks rather than at the possibilities	0	5	15	20
I would rather look at reality than an imagined future	0	5	15	20
It is more important to be correct than adventurous in thinking	0	5	15	20
Planning in detail is more effective than rushing to a decision	0	5	15	20
Before going into a big meeting I like to cover all the bases	0	5	15	20
I like sticking to the rules	0	5	15	20
Failure is not trying rather than not succeeding	20	15	5	0
Total for Opportunity / Fear				

Category 3	Always	Most of the time	On occasion	Never
I find it easier to relate to people than to technology	20	15	5	0
I tend to prefer group decisions over individual leadership	20	15	5	0
Making up my own mind is generally more effective than consulting with the team	0	5	15	20
People should behave in accordance with corporate objectives, rather than determine their own goals	0	5	15	20
Rules of operation are more important than freedom of choice	0	5	15	20
Teams need rules as they will tend to become inefficient if given too much freedom	0	5	15	20
I tend to ask closed and leading questions in order to speed up the process	0	5	15	20
I am happy working on my own and don't need others	0	5	15	20
If I let my guard down people may take advantage of me	0	5	15	20
Total for Trust / Control				

Category 4	Always	Most of the time	On occasion	Never
My friends/colleagues would say I do things with other peoples' interests at heart	20	15	5	0
Sometimes I find it hard to find a balance between my personal needs and those of my team	20	15	5	0
I assume everyone else is most interested in looking after their own needs	0	5	15	20
I am motivated to understand my buyers' needs rather than sell them my ideas	20	15	5	0
I listen to the views of my team members rather than impart my own	20	15	5	0
I can trust my team to make decisions about new and complex problems	20	15	5	0
When I challenge someone's thinking it is always in order to help them, rather than to promote my opinion	20	15	5	0
I start conversations with a question rather than a statement	20	15	5	0
I challenge people with what I know	0	5	15	20
Total for Your needs / My needs				

Category 5	Always	Most of the time	On occasion	Never
When making decisions I tend to react with 'gut' feeling	20	15	5	0
I like to know what my colleagues are thinking	0	5	15	20
My friends/colleagues view me as a highly rational person	0	5	15	20
I prefer to deal with someone in person rather than in writing	20	15	5	0
I am more comfortable with facts than feelings	0	5	15	20
If I get a 'gut' feeling about a business decision, or an intuitive reaction to a person, I do not ignore it	20	15	5	0
My friends/colleagues view me as a compassionate person	20	15	5	0
My colleagues would see me as open and caring	20	15	5	0
I worry about how my team is feeling	20	15	5	0
Total for Feelings / Facts				

Category 6	Always	Most of the time	On occasion	Never
I like to get one thing done before moving to another	0	5	15	20
I like to have a to-do list	0	5	15	20
My staff view me as easy going	20	15	5	0
I do not mind being unprepared for meetings	20	15	5	0
I prefer to have regular rather than impromptu meetings	0	5	15	20
When going on holiday, I tend to have detailed travel plans	0	5	15	20
My personal preference is not to have an open-door policy to staff, but to have regular meetings	0	5	15	20
I prefer not to have an agenda for meetings	20	15	5	0
I am an organised thinker	0	5	15	20
Total for Free flowing / Organised				

Category 7	Always	Most of the time	On occasion	Never
If something is not broken I tend to leave it as it is	0	5	15	20
I tend to judge my performance against that of other people	0	5	15	20
I like to be sure we will win assignments and just doing our best is not enough	0	5	15	20
I am motivated to better myself more than to worry about how others are performing	20	15	5	0
I am motivated to be the highest performer in my team	0	5	15	20
I tend to ask people to justify ideas first before agreeing with them	0	5	15	20
I am more interested in what someone can do for me than I am in what I can do for them	0	5	15	20
I am an optimistic person	20	15	5	0
Knowing what my competition is doing is more important than just focusing on my own performance	0	5	15	20
Total for My best / Better than you				

Category 8	Always	Most of the time	On occasion	Never
I like to work at doing the same thing better before moving on to doing different things	0	5	15	20
I think the best ideas come from thinking about them	0	5	15	20
Leadership should be done by the most senior person	0	5	15	20
I tend to get other people to attend to the detail of decisions while I deal with the big picture	20	15	5	0
Dreams are great but reality is more important	0	5	15	20
I like to make sure things are perfect rather than just OK	0	5	15	20
People seek me out for what I know more than how I interact	0	5	15	20
People say I have lots of ideas, but they see many of them as unrealistic	20	15	5	0
I tend to have ideas without any obvious rationale	20	15	5	0
Total for Big picture / Detail				

Calculating and interpreting your score

Take the scores above and insert them in this table.

Category	Total score per above	Behaviour
1		Leading / Following
2		Opportunity / Fear
3		Trust / Control
4		Your needs / My needs
5		Feelings / Facts
6		Free flowing / Organised
7		My best / Better than you
8		Big picture / Detail

Now get a pen and mark your score on the Octagon™ below. This will give you an overall picture of how you behave.

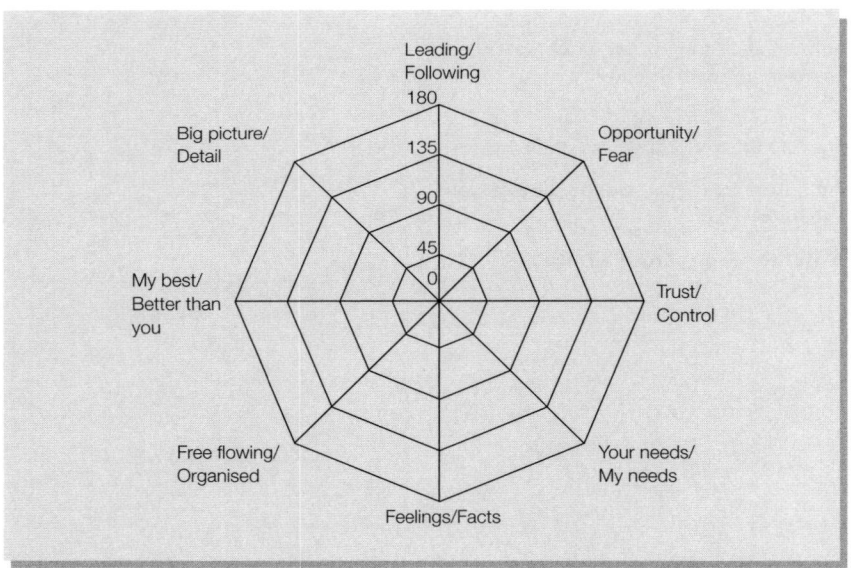

Appendix 2: Your Octagon™ action plan

A process for planning your actions

1 Look at each behaviour in detail, one at a time.

2 Decide whether you are comfortable with your results.

3 If you are then move on to the next behaviour. If you are not then write down in the boxes provided your score and the score you would like to achieve – and the date by when you would like to achieve it.

4 Next, look at the suggestions we have included for making a change in that behaviour and think about how these suggestions may apply to you, in your environment.

5 Decide on small things you can do and write them in the next box. We advise small things, because these are more likely to get done than big things.

6 Decide on who, if anyone, you would like to help you work on those behavioural changes.

7 Move on to the next behaviour and repeat the process.

1 Leading / Following

If you score over 140 then buyers will notice that you tend to be the first to say things. You might be perceived by some buyers as too directive. You may be seen by buyers as not listening enough to them.

If you score around or below 40 then buyers may see that you tend only to say things if specifically asked. You might be perceived by buyers as lacking in ideas or thoughts of your own or lacking the confidence to put them forward.

180

⇐ *You are always the first to say something in a meeting and possibly in a way that does not solicit challenge*

⇐ *You will put forward your thoughts, but in a non-'final' way*

⇐ *You will wait to see what people say and then say something*

⇐ *You will ask if anyone has any ideas and then put forward your own*

⇐ *You will ask for other people to make suggestions and then add to them*

⇐ *You will ask others for input and then get others to add on*

⇐ *You will ask others for input and then be quiet*

⇐ *When asked you will be happy to put forward your ideas*

⇐ *You will only say something when asked and even then will answer with a question*

⇐ *You rarely say anything in the meeting, certainly never to challenge*

0

Self-score: [ ]   *Desired score:* [ ]   *By when:* [ ]

To raise your score

▪ Say what you think – and don't worry about what people might think

▪ Make suggestions even if you think that a good answer has already been put forward

▪ Use closed or leading questions to speed up the process

▪ Start a meeting by asking if anyone has anything to say.

To lower your score

- Even when the room is silent resist the temptation to be the first to speak

- When you ask a question make sure it is a genuine open question rather than a rhetorical or leading question

- Don't answer your own questions

- When someone else asks a question, rather than answer it yourself, ask others what they think

- Before saying something ask yourself if what you are about to say adds value to the topic in hand – and if it does not then say nothing.

Things you will try to do:

Who would you like to help you?

2 Opportunity / Fear

If you score over 140 then buyers will see that you tend to see the positive in things. You may however be perceived by a buyer as someone who is unrealistic, maybe a little reckless and too prepared to try things that have not been well thought through.

If you score around or below 40 then the buyer will see that you tend to be concerned about the risks of new ideas. You may be perceived by a buyer as someone who spends a lot of time talking about the problems and dangers of an idea rather than the potential upside of resolving the issue.

180

⇐ *You are always optimistic, sometimes unrealistically so*

⇐ *You are always happy to get involved in new ideas/ventures regardless of risk*

⇐ *You like new ideas that have been well thought out*

⇐ *You are the pragmatic one, balancing risk and reward*

⇐ *You are happy to support new, well thought out ideas, but would not get involved yourself*

⇐ *You will get involved in new ideas, but only once convinced that the risks are small*

⇐ *You naturally doubt most things can work*

⇐ *You will not get involved in anything that has not already been tried and tested*

0

Self-score: ⬚   *Desired score:* ⬚   *By when:* ⬚

To raise your score

▪ At meetings, use brainstorming techniques and allow no challenges – however wild the ideas may be

▪ Next time you are about to say 'but' – stop yourself

▪ Periodically try doing something completely new without calculating the risk

▪ Draw up a list of the pros and cons of a project, making sure there are equal numbers on both sides

- Next time you have an idea suggest it to someone before you start questioning it.

To lower your score

- Draw up a list of the pros and cons of a project, making sure there are equal numbers on both sides
- Before you put forward a new idea imagine the positive and negative impact on the short term, the medium term and the long term.

Things you will try to do:

Who would you like to help you?

---

3 Trust / Control

If you score over 140 then buyers will see that you naturally tend to trust people. You may however be perceived by buyers as too hands-off, even disinterested.

If you score around or below 40 then buyers will feel that you tend to stay in control. You may be viewed by buyers as driving conversations and the relationship and not listening and letting them do the driving.

180

⇐ *You can be seen as the absent leader*

⇐ *You allocate tasks and then don't get in touch until the project is done*

⇐ *You find yourself making excuses for people*

⇐ *You develop a set of people to whom you can 'abdicate' responsibility*

⇐ *You are seen as the core of the team*

⇐ *You keep an eye on what people are doing, but with care*

⇐ *You are very clear and specific at the delegation stage*

⇐ *You are constantly checking what people are doing*

⇐ *You are seen as independent within a team*

⇐ *You work on your own and not in teams*

⇐ *You don't delegate*

0

Self-score: [ ]   *Desired score:* [ ]   *By when:* [ ]

To raise your score

■ Delegate a task that is low risk and see what happens

■ When delegating a task make objectives and deadlines clear, and then do not get in touch until the deadline has passed

■ Ask to have a task within a team, and don't question other team members' tasks

■ Do something which clearly shows that you are trusting someone with something very important to you

- Explain that you will not be reviewing something you are delegating – that you trust them to get it right

- When you know you will not be able to do something, say so at the outset.

To lower your score

- Put dates in your diary for checking on progress – and then check

- Ask team members how much they would like you to be involved.

Things you will try to do:

Who would you like to help you?

---

4 Your needs / My needs

If you score over 140 then buyers will feel that you are trying to help them – even at your own expense. However, whilst seeing you as helpful, some buyers may see you as not being as self-confident as you could be.

If you score around or below 40 then buyers will feel that you tend to do things only if there is something in it for you. Buyers may perceive selfish motives in your actions and feel that you do not listen to their needs sufficiently.

180

⇦ *You will put yourself out to a significant extent to make sure other people are OK*

⇦ *You will compromise yourself in the interests of the team*

⇦ *You will give recognition to all and seek none yourself*

⇦ *You will facilitate a meeting to make sure everyone has had their issues covered*

⇦ *You like to be part of a team recognised for achievement*

⇦ *You will seek recognition for tasks completed*

⇦ *You will drive projects and meetings according to your agenda only*

⇦ *You don't understand why people do things if they do not further your objectives*

0

Self-score: [ ]   *Desired score:* [ ]   *By when:* [ ]

To raise your score

▪ Do something simple which clearly helps someone else but has little or no value for you

▪ One day a week, consciously do something that is not for your own benefit

▪ Ask someone what they personally want to get out of a project

▪ Challenge people to develop their own personal development plans.

To lower your score

- When delegating, recognise that the other person prefers a different approach, but be clear that in this case your priorities are more important
- Be public about the personal things you need to do and block your diary accordingly (gym, children etc.)
- Make sure you do at least one thing each day that is purely for you.

Things you will try to do:

Who would you like to help you?

5 Feelings / Facts

If you score over 140 then buyers will see you as being fair. Some buyers may however see you as too 'touchy-feely' and more concerned with the well-being of people than on making money.

If you score around or below 40 then you may not be able to engage well with buyers. You may be perceived by some buyers as cold, unfeeling and inconsiderate of others.

180

⇐ *You deal with people based on what is fair*

⇐ *You like to share your feelings with your team*

⇐ *You make sure people are happy with what they are doing*

⇐ *You deal with people based on the balance of fair and logical*

⇐ *You like to know about your team's personal situation, but do not share your own*

⇐ *You will put up with people talking about their personal situation, but will not remember it*

⇐ *You only deal in facts, not emotions*

⇐ *You deal with people based on what makes sense*

0

Self-score: [   ]   *Desired score:* [   ]   *By when:* [   ]

To raise your score

- Ask someone how they are feeling about something
- Talk about something personal about you
- Ask people about the impact decisions will have on them
- Look people in the eye when talking to them
- When speaking to people give them your complete attention
- Focus on remembering people's names when you meet them for the first time.

To lower your score

- Ask about business objectives when delegating tasks
- When you are considering the impact an action may have on a person, match it with the impact on the business
- Don't open up about personal things unless specifically asked to
- Ask people about the efficiency or profitability of things.

Things you will try to do:

Who would you like to help you?

6 Free flowing / Organised

If you score over 140 then buyers will see that you are prepared to go with the flow. Some buyers may also see you as somewhat disorganised.

If you score around or below 40 then buyers will see that you like to plan things out well in advance. The danger here is that buyers may see you as being too focused on the plan and that sometimes you lose sight of the objectives. They may also believe that you are not adaptable enough to changing circumstances.

180

⇐ *You feel constrained by schedules*

⇐ *You tend to have last-minute mayhem before deadlines*

⇐ *You don't understand why others cannot be as flexible as you*

⇐ *You like to have a timetable, but it needs some flexibility built into it*

⇐ *You like to have a broad plan of where the project is going*

⇐ *You get very frustrated by people not sticking to their deadlines*

⇐ *You always have work finished ahead of deadlines*

⇐ *You think an agenda is crucial to a successful meeting*

0

Self-score: [ ]   Desired score: [ ]   By when: [ ]

To raise your score

▨ Have one regular meeting each week without an agenda

▨ Next time you go on holiday just book the flights and don't worry about every night's accommodation

▨ Use brainstorming or mind mapping as techniques for running meetings rather than 'interrogative' questions

▨ Cancel standard meetings in lieu of only having one when it becomes important.

To lower your score

- Have a to-do list and don't go home until you have finished it
- Always have a shopping list – and use it
- Always have an agenda
- Complete a formal meeting planner before each meeting.

Things you will try to do:

Who would you like to help you?

---

7 My best / Better than you

If you score over 140 then buyers will see that you are driven to achieve the best result possible. Some buyers may however feel that you are self-centred and overly ambitious.

If you score around or below 40 then buyers will see you are driven by making sure that no-one else will achieve better results. You may be seen as worrying too much about beating the competition, rather than focusing on achieving the best possible result.

180

⇦ *You focus entirely on being the best you can be*

⇦ *You make sure that you learn from everyone else*

⇦ *As long as you are improving you are happy for others to do so as well*

⇦ *Others doing well drives you to do better*

⇦ *You want to create your own best practice*

⇦ *You want to know what the current best practice is and then be better than it*

⇦ *Others doing well drives you to find out how*

⇦ *You are happy to see others fail*

⇦ *The key is making sure you win*

0

Self-score: [ ]   *Desired score:* [ ]   *By when:* [ ]

To raise your score

▪ Don't say negative things about other people

▪ Take up a hobby where there can be no winner

▪ Do one thing a day where you need to beat your own personal best

▪ Next time someone comes up with an idea just acknowledge how good it is and do not challenge or add on.

To lower your score

- Do a competitor analysis before taking on any project
- When planning something always ask what a competitor or colleague would do in the same situation
- Take up a competitive sport and strive to win
- When someone else comes up with a new idea consider if there is a way that you think it could be improved.

Things you will try to do:

Who would you like to help you?

---

8 Big picture / Detail

If you score over 140 then buyers will see that you can engage in their strategy and vision. You may be seen by some buyers as someone who does not pay enough attention to the details.

If you score around or below 40 then buyers will see that you understand the details and reality of the situation. Some buyers may feel you have a tendency to get bogged down in the detail.

180

⇐ *You like to think about vision and dreams*

⇐ *You get bored with conversations about detail*

⇐ *You like concepts*

⇐ *You like to make sure that vision, strategy and action are aligned*

⇐ *You like to deal with what needs to be done*

⇐ *You get frustrated with unrealistic ideas*

⇐ *You like to look at the detail of the current situation*

⇐ *Things need to be perfect – now*

0

Self-score: ☐ Desired score: ☐ By when: ☐

To raise your score

■ Before making a suggestion question yourself as to whether this will have a significant impact on the project as a whole

■ Ask yourself whether a specific action is material

■ Talk about vision and strategy

■ Next time you are tempted to ask about a detail in a project – stop yourself.

To lower your score

■ Challenge people who talk about vision and dreams to make sure their idea will work and that more pressing concerns are dealt with first

■ Cross-check all numbers in your documents before passing them on for review

- Check the spelling in every document
- In every meeting ask one question about detail
- Make a point of picking one small error in everything you review.

Things you will try to do:

Who would you like to help you?

Appendix 3: Buyer Feedback Tool

To the successful I Owe U salesperson, any feedback from buyers is hugely valuable. It helps them to adjust their approach and avoid becoming complacent or slipping into bad habits.

The Buyer Feedback Tool below can be used in two ways:

■ sent to buyers for them to complete

■ used as the framework for a face-to-face discussion.

If used as a discussion framework, you should consider having someone other than the key sales contact collect the feedback. Buyers are often more honest about the primary salesperson's behaviour when talking to a second person.

Name of primary sales contact			
Dates and nature of recent purchases or contact			
Frequency of communication	Too frequent	Appropriate	Infrequent – would prefer more regular contact
What do you see as the salesperson's three key strengths?	1. 2. 3.		
What are three things that the salesperson could do to improve?	1. 2. 3.		
What else would you like us to know about the way we work with you?			

Here is an example of a completed Buyer Feedback Tool:

Name of primary sales contact	Jeremy MacIntosh
Dates and nature of recent purchases or contact	Mid June 2006 New server October 2006 New HR software
Frequency of communication	~~Too frequent~~ (Appropriate) ~~Infrequent – would prefer more regular contact~~ I only call him when I need him
What do you see as the salesperson's three key strengths?	1 He turns up when I call him 2 He seems to understand his stuff 3 His price is always competitive
What are three things that the salesperson could do to improve?	1 I guess he could keep me posted on what his company is developing 2 I would like to know a bit more about what other companies are doing. I don't know what I don't know 3 I'm not sure my people are using the HR software in the most effective way. He could offer us some tips on how to get the most from the system.
What else would you like us to know about the way we work with you?	At present I only use you when I think I need you, and that has been my decision. I suspect I would get more value if I could learn more about what opportunities there may be for me to use technology where I am not aware of it

Appendix 4: Blank planning sheets

Understanding your relationship with a key buyer

Name of buyer	
Who called the meeting?	
Why did that person call the meeting?	
Think of five discussion points that you initiated in the meeting	
Think of five discussion points that the buyer initiated in the meeting	
What was said to wrap up the meeting – by both of you?	

Planning form for taking your buyer through the different levels of thinking

Name of buyer company	*Name of buyer individual*	
Possible level 1 issues at present		
Possible questions to create level 4	a b c	
Possible level 4 situation	a b c	

Appendix 5: Recognising SHAPE questions

Below are some exercises to help you learn more about the questions and the buyer responses. After each exercise is an answer sheet.

Don't beat yourself up if you don't get this 100% correct. It takes a lot of practice, and we thought you might like to start that practice now.

Exercise 1

Which of these is a **Surface** and which is a **Hunt** question?

	S	H
1 When did you last appoint your advisors?		
2 Do you have any difficulties projecting where you'll be in five years?		
3 What internal legal capability do you have?		
4 Do you find it hard to control inventory?		
5 How satisfied are you with the current equipment?		
6 What is the most frustrating aspect of the current offering?		
7 What's the structure of your organisation?		
8 What system do you use to determine the equipment you should use?		
9 Does the poor communication lead to other problems?		
10 What sort of microwave do you have at present?		

Exercise 2

Read each statement and decide whether it represents a Fact, a Challenge or an Outcome statement by the buyer.

	F	C	O
1 We need a to have a faster turnaround			
2 I have trouble with file management			
3 Our debtors pay very slowly			
4 We're using so many providers in our business			
5 I'm very dissatisfied with our ability to resolve issues quickly			
6 We'd like to increase our productivity			
7 We want to improve our buyer feedback			
8 There seem to be faster systems in the market			
9 I need an oven which has a very accurate thermometer			
10 Our staff turnover is too high for our business			

Exercise 3

Which of these is a Hunt and which is a Paint question?

	H	P
1 If you could get a reply in 48 hours how would it help?		
2 Does this ever affect your ability to meet deadlines?		
3 How much do these delays cost you in excess labour?		
4 What value would speeding up the process have?		
5 How do delays affect your ability to resolve issues?		
6 Would you be interested in a way to track projects?		
7 Might you miss an opportunity because you cannot produce fast enough?		
8 Is the occasional short-circuit of the freezer causing you any problems?		
9 How much more business could you generate if we could reduce delays in processing by 30 days?		
10 Would staff motivation increase if you were able to have no down-time?		

Answers to Exercise 1

	S	H
1 When did you last appoint your advisors?	✓	
2 Do you have any difficulties projecting where you'll be in five years?		✓
3 What internal legal capability do you have?	✓	
4 Do you find it hard to control inventory?		✓
5 How satisfied are you with the current equipment?	✓	
6 What is the most frustrating aspect of the current offering?		✓
7 What's the structure of your organisation?	✓	
8 What system do you use to determine the equipment you should use?	✓	
9 Does the poor communication lead to other problems?		✓
10 What sort of microwave do you have at present?	✓	

Bear in mind that the key rule here is that a hunt question is likely to solicit a problem or challenge whereas a surface question is likely to solicit a fact.

Answers to Exercise 2

	F	C	O
1 We need a to have a faster turnaround			✓
2 I have trouble with file management		✓	
3 Our debtors pay very slowly	✓		
4 We're using so many providers in our business	✓		
5 I'm very dissatisfied with our ability to resolve issues quickly		✓	
6 We'd like to increase our productivity			✓
7 We want to improve our buyer feedback			✓
8 There seem to be faster systems in the market	✓		
9 I need an oven which has a very accurate thermometer			✓
10 Our staff turnover is too high for our business		✓	

You might argue that some of the facts above are challenges. They may be in your mind, but the point is – are they a challenge in the buyer's mind? You should ask a further hunt question to get confirmation that it is a challenge. Again, a challenge is current and negative, a need is future and positive.

Answers to Exercise 3

	H	P
1 If you could get a reply in 48 hours how would it help?		✓
2 Does this ever affect your ability to meet deadlines?	✓	
3 How much do these delays cost you in excess labour?	✓	
4 What value would speeding up the process have?		✓
5 How do delays affect your ability to resolve issues?	✓	
6 Would you be interested in a way to track projects?		✓
7 Might you miss an opportunity because you cannot produce fast enough?	✓	
8 Is the occasional short-circuit of the freezer causing you any problems?	✓	
9 How much more business could you generate if we could reduce delays in processing by 30 days?		✓
10 Would staff motivation increase if you were able to have no down-time?		✓

Hunt questions point to the current negative situation, paint questions point to a positive future.

You should now feel more comfortable that you understand the type of questions that correspond to each stage of the SHAPE process. The next stage of your development is to practise your questioning style so that it becomes natural.

Index

OTHER BESTSELLING SMARTER BOOKS

ISBN-10: 0-273-70613-6
ISBN-13: 978-0-273-70613-7
Price: £ 22.00
Format: 234X156
Extent: 232 pp

Smarter Pricing

What is it really worth? How much will customers pay? Where will our competitors respond?

From airline tickets to bottled water, price can have a profound impact in the market.

Smarter Pricing will help you to make more intelligent pricing decisions, implement pricing strategies and structures more effectively in the market and capture more value for your business, so you too can become a market leader.

10: 0-273-70560-1
978-0-273-70560-4
99
56

Smarter Outsourcing

Outsourcing is a central issue for companies large and small, but few of us truly have the knowledge on how to decide what should be outsourced and how to do it.

Smarter Outsourcing will ensure you have all the knowledge you need for long-term success and ongoing commitment from your clients and providers no matter what industry you work in.

s. Giving you the business skills you need to succeed.

lable from all good bookshops; or buy
at www.pearson-books.com